Determining Sample Size

P O C K E T G U I D E S T O
SOCIAL WORK RESEARCH METHODS

Series Editor
Tony Tripodi, DSW
Professor Emeritus, Ohio State University

Determining Sample Size
Balancing Power, Precision, and Practicality
Patrick Dattalo

PATRICK DATTALO

Determining
Sample
Size

Balancing Power, Precision, and Practicality

OXFORD
UNIVERSITY PRESS

2008

OXFORD
UNIVERSITY PRESS

Oxford University Press, Inc., publishes works that further
Oxford University's objective of excellence
in research, scholarship, and education.

Oxford   New York
Auckland   Cape Town   Dar es Salaam   Hong Kong   Karachi
Kuala Lumpur   Madrid   Melbourne   Mexico City   Nairobi
New Delhi   Shanghai   Taipei   Toronto

With offices in
Argentina   Austria   Brazil   Chile   Czech Republic   France   Greece
Guatemala   Hungary   Italy   Japan   Poland   Portugal   Singapore
South Korea   Switzerland   Thailand   Turkey   Ukraine   Vietnam

Copyright © 2008 by Oxford University Press, Inc.

Published by Oxford University Press, Inc.
198 Madison Avenue, New York, New York 10016

www.oup.com

Oxford is a registered trademark of Oxford University Press

Library of Congress Cataloging-in-Publication Data
Dattalo, Patrick
Determining sample size : balancing power,
precision, and practicality / Patrick Dattalo
p.cm.—(Pocket guides to social work research methods)
Includes bibliographical references and index.
ISBN 978-0-19-531549-3
1. Sampling (Statistics)   2. Social sciences—Statistical methods.
3. Social surveys—Methodology.   I. Title.
HA31.2D38 2008
Sampling (Statistics—dc22   2007033289

1 3 5 7 9 8 6 4 2
Printed in the United States of America
on acid-free paper

For Debra,
Lucevan li occhi suoi più che la stella.

Contents

Determining Sample Size

1

Basic Terms and Concepts

Sample size determination is an important and often difficult step in planning an empirical study. Sampling theory and practice have been extensively discussed, and, therefore, the following is a brief review of some of the most important sampling-related concepts. For a comprehensive review of sampling, see Cochran (1977), Fink (2002), and Kish (1965). For a discussion of sampling within the context of research design, see Rubin and Babbie (2005).

An *element* is a unit (e.g., person, object) of a population. A *population* is a theoretically specified aggregation of elements. The cost of studying an entire population is usually prohibitive to both researchers and those being studied in terms of privacy, time, and money. Therefore, a subset of a given population must be selected; this is called sampling. *Sampling* is a strategy used to select elements from a population. A *sample* is a subset of the population elements that results from a sampling strategy. Ideally, a sample is selected that is representative of a population (i.e., elements accurately portray characteristics of the population). A *sampling frame* is the list, index, or records from which the sample will be drawn, which might not be totally inclusive of the study population. Because sampling is the process of selecting population elements to study, sample **design** addresses two basic issues:

(1) how elements of the population will be selected and (2) how many elements will be selected.

Selecting Elements From a Population

The ultimate goal of sample design is to select a set of elements from a population in such a way that descriptions of those elements accurately portray characteristics of the population (parameters) from which they were selected. Another important goal of sample design is to yield maximum precision (i.e., minimum variance) per unit cost. To achieve these goals, researchers typically rely on probability sampling, in which every element in the population has a known chance of being selected into the sample. *Probability sampling* allows the chance of an element being selected to be quantified (ideally equal). Probability sampling strategies, through statistical procedures, allow estimates of sampling error to be calculated.

There are a variety of probability sampling strategies. Frequently used probability sampling strategies are *simple, systematic, stratified,* and *cluster* sampling. **Simple random sampling** may be the best known sampling strategy. A commonly used simple random sampling procedure is to assign a number to each element in the sampling frame and use an unbiased process, such as a random number generator, to select elements from the sampling frame. Random number generators are included in some commercial software and are available free on the Internet (e.g., http://www.random.org).

Systematic random sampling uses a list of population elements. If elements can be assumed to be randomly listed, then a starting point is randomly identified, and elements are selected using a sampling interval. These intervals are calculated by dividing the desired sample size by the number of elements in the sampling frame. For example, to select a sample size of 50 from a sampling frame with 100 elements, pick a random starting point and select every second element until 50 elements are selected.

Stratified sampling uses groups to achieve representativeness, or to ensure that a certain number of elements from each group are selected. In a stratified sample, the sampling frame is divided into nonoverlapping groups or strata (e.g., age groups, gender). Then a random sample is taken from each stratum. This technique, for example, can be used to study a small subgroup of a population that could be excluded in a simple random sample.

Cluster sampling enables random sampling from either a very large population or one that is geographically diverse. An important objective of cluster sampling is to reduce costs by increasing sampling efficiency. A problem with cluster sampling is that, although every cluster has the same chance of being selected, elements within large clusters have a greatly reduced chance of being selected in the final sample. Using the probability proportionate to size (PPS) technique corrects this error. PPS takes into account the difference in cluster size and adjusts the chance that clusters will be selected. That is, PPS increases the odds that elements in larger clusters will be selected.

Random sampling can be difficult to achieve because of time, cost, and ethical considerations. Therefore, it is often necessary to use other sampling techniques, often labeled nonrandom or *nonprobability sampling*. With nonprobability sampling, elements of the population have an unknown chance of being selected. At best, nonrandom sampling strategies can yield a sample that is representative (i.e., portrays key characteristics) of a population. At worst, nonrandom sampling strategies can yield a nonrepresentative sample with an unknown amount of error. Commonly used nonprobability sampling strategies are *availability, snowball,* and *quota* sampling.

Availability sampling is a technique in which elements are selected because of their accessibility to the researcher. A criticism of this technique is that bias is introduced into the sample. Volunteers always are suspect because they might not be representative of the overall population. An example of an availability, or convenience, sample is one in which participants are selected from the clinic, facility, or educational institution at which the researcher is employed. Bias is likely to be introduced using this sampling technique because of the methods, styles, and preferences of treatment employed at a given facility.

Purposive sampling involves the use of the researcher's knowledge of the population in terms of research goals. That is, elements are selected based on the researcher's judgment that they will provide access to the desired information. For example, sometimes purposive sampling is used to select typical cases, and sometimes it is used to select atypical cases. Purposive sampling also can be used to select participants based on their willingness to be studied or on their knowledge of a particular topic.

Quota sampling is a nonprobability version of stratified sampling. The distinguishing feature of a quota sample is that guidelines are set to ensure that the sample represents certain characteristics in proportion to their prevalence in the population.

Snowball sampling is sampling from a known network. Snowball sampling is used to identify participants when appropriate candidates for study are difficult to locate. For example, if locating an adequate number of profoundly deaf people is difficult, a profoundly deaf person who participates in a local support group could be recruited to assist in locating other profoundly deaf people willing to participate in a study. In other words, it is possible to have known members of a population help identify other members of their population.

Deciding How Many Elements to Select From a Population

Because a sample is only part of a population, generalization from a sample to a population usually involves error. There are two basic types of error that can occur in the process of generalizing from a sample to a population: sampling, or random, error and nonsampling, or systematic, error (SE). The latter type of error also is called *bias*.

Sampling error results from the "luck of the draw": too many elements of one kind and not enough elements of another kind. As sample size increases, SE decreases, albeit slowly. If the population is relatively homogeneous, SE will be small. Heterogeneity can be estimated from random sample data, using the standard deviation or an analogous statistic.

Nonsampling error is often a more serious problem than SE, because nonsampling error cannot be controlled by increasing sample size (Cuddeback, Wilson, Orme, & Combs-Orme, 2004). Nonsampling can be organized into three categories: (1) *Selection bias* is the systematic tendency to exclude some elements from the sample. With an availability sample, selection bias is a major concern. In contrast, with a well-designed probability sample, selection bias is minimal. (2) *Nonresponse bias* is present to the extent that respondents and nonrespondents differ on variables of interest, and extrapolation from respondents to nonrespondents will be problematic. (3) *Response bias* occurs when respondents "shade the truth" because of interviewer attitudes, the wording of questions, or the juxtaposition of questions.

The size of a sample is an important element in determining the statistical precision with which population values can be estimated. In general, increased sample size is associated with decreased sampling error. The larger the sample, the more likely the results are to represent the population. However, the relationship between sampling error and sample size is not simple or proportional. There are diminishing returns associated with adding elements to a sample.

In summary, the cost of studying an entire population usually is prohibitive to both researchers and those being studied in terms of privacy, time, and money. Consequently, a subset or sample of a given population must be selected. An important goal of sampling is to provide a practical and economic mechanism to enable extrapolation from a sample to a population. This book focuses on quantitative research in which a primary goal is to seek evidence about a characteristic or a relationship and to use statistical inference to generalize obtained results from a sample to a population. More specifically, the focus here is on frequentist methods for determining sample size. The term *frequentist* is used to describe those approaches that assume that probability is a long-term frequency. Bayesian strategies are considered an alternative to frequentist approaches (e.g., see Gill, 2002). Adopting a Bayesian paradigm requires the assumption that probability is a subjective phenomenon.

A detailed discussion of Bayesian probability theory is beyond the scope of this book. Only procedures that assume a frequentist approach to probability are considered. For a discussion of Bayesian strategies and a comparison with frequentist methods, see Adcock (1997). An effective sample design requires the balancing of several important criteria: (1) achieving research objectives, (2) providing accurate estimates of sampling variability, (3) being feasible, and (4) maximizing economy (i.e., achieving research objectives for minimum cost). These four criteria can conflict, and researchers must seek a balance among them.

This book is organized as follows:

1. approaches to estimating sample size, including
   a. power analysis
   b. confidence intervals
   c. computer-intensive methods
   d. ethical and cost considerations
2. synthesis and recommendations
3. comprehensive worked examples
4. annotated bibliography of recommended readings and resources for sample size determination.

See Table 1.1 for a summary of discussion and examples by procedure. See Table 1.2 for a summary of effect-size measures discussed in subsequent chapters. It is assumed that readers are familiar with issues related to the appropriate application of each statistical procedure in terms of assumptions and purpose. Interested readers should refer to the appendix for an annotated bibliography of additional resources.

Table 1.1 Summary of Discussion and Examples by Procedure

Procedure	Discussion-Power Analysis	Discussion-Confidence Intervals	Power Analysis Example	Confidence Interval Example
Difference Two Means	Chapter 2	Chapter 3	Chapter 6, Examples 1, 2	Chapter 6, Examples 1, 2
Difference Two Proportions	Chapter 2	Chapter 3	Chapter 6, Example 3	Chapter 6, Example 3
Odds Ratio	Chapter 2	Chapter 3	Chapter 6, Example 4	Chapter 6, Example 4
Chi Square	Chapter 2	Chapter 3	Chapter 6, Example 5	Chapter 6, Example 5
ANOVA/ ANCOVA/ Repeated Measures	Chapter 2	Chapter 3	Chapter 6, Examples 6, 7a, 7b, 8	Chapter 6, Examples 6, 7a, 7b, 8
MANOVA/ MANCOVA/ Repeated Measures	Chapter 2	Chapter 3	Chapter 6, Examples 9, 10, 11	Chapter 6, Examples 9, 10, 11
Correlation	Chapter 2	Chapter 3	Chapter 6, Example 12	Chapter 6, Example 12
Regression	Chapter 2	Chapter 3	Chapter 6, Example 13	Chapter 6, Example 13
Discriminant Function Analysis	Chapter 2	Chapter 3	Chapter 6, Example 14	Chapter 6, Example 14
Logistic Regression	Chapter 2	Chapter 3	Chapter 6, Example 15	Chapter 6, Example 15
Cox Regression	Chapter 2	Chapter 3	Chapter 6, Example 16	Chapter 6, Example 16
Structural Equation Modeling	Chapter 2	Chapter 3	Chapter 6, Example 17	Chapter 6, Example 17
Multilevel Analysis	Chapter 2	Chapter 3	Chapter 6, Example 18	Chapter 6, Example 18
Computer-Intensive Methods	Chapter 5	Chapter 5	Chapter 5	Chapter 5
Effect Size	Chapter 2	Chapter 3	Chapter 6, Example 19	Chapter 6, Example 19

Table 1.2 Small, Medium, and Large Values of Cohen's Effect Sizes

Effect Size	Small	Medium	Large
d	.20	.50	.80
r	.10	.30	.50
w	.10	.30	.50
f	.10	.25	.40
f^2	.02	.15	.35

2

Statistical Power Analysis

A s discussed in chapter 1, the focus of this book is on quantitative research in which a primary goal is to seek evidence about a
characteristic or relationship (ideally, a causal relationship) and to use
statistical inference to generalize obtained results to a population. The
costs, in terms of privacy, time, and money, of collecting data on an
entire population usually is excessive both to researchers and study
participants.

Because the sample is only part of the whole, generalization usually
involves error. The importance of sampling error is clarified if it is
assumed that the ultimate goal of sampling is to provide evidence of
causal relationships in a population. Cook and Campbell (1979) explain
that, according to the nineteenth-century philosopher John Stuart Mill,
at least three criteria must be met to justify causal claims: (1) association
(correlation or the cause is related to the effect), (2) temporality (the
cause comes before the effect), and (3) elimination of plausible alternative explanations (other plausible explanations for an effect are considered and ruled out).

Cook and Campbell (1979) use the term *validity* to refer to the best
available approximation of the truth or falsity of propositions, including
propositions about cause. Cook and Campbell identify four types of

validity. These are *construct validity, internal validity, statistical conclusion validity,* and *external validity*. **Construct validity** refers to whether the measures used in a study actually measure what they purport to measure. **Internal validity** refers to the strength of the causal linkages between and among independent and dependent variables. **External validity** refers to the ability to generalize a study's results to other times, places, and persons. **Statistical conclusion validity** refers to the ability to presume covariation between or among variables given a specified alpha level and the observed amount of dispersion in a sample.

The priority among validity types varies with the kind of research being conducted. Statistical conclusion validity is perhaps most directly related to sampling. According to Cook and Campbell (1979), issues or problems that affect statistical conclusion validity are as follows:

1. Research design
2. The criterion for statistical significance (level of alpha or type I error)
3. Population variance in the criterion variable
4. Magnitude of the difference between the actual value of the tested parameter and the value specified by the null hypothesis (effect size)
5. Type of hypothesis (one-tailed or directional versus two-tailed or nondirectional)
6. Types of statistical test used (e.g., *t*-test versus sign test)
7. Sample size

The remaining portion of this text focuses on sample size as an important and controllable influence on the statistical precision or sampling error with which population values can be estimated. In general, increased sample size is associated with decreased sampling error. The larger the sample, the more likely it is that the results will validly represent the population. However, the relationship between sampling error and sample size is not simple and proportionate. There are diminishing returns associated with adding elements to a sample. In most applied research settings, however, limited resources restrict the number of individuals that can be sampled.

It is hoped that the following discussion will provide beginning reference points for sample size determination and encourage researchers to continue to search for resolutions to often difficult sample-size decisions. For instance, when designing a study, researchers should be prepared to grapple with the difficult trade-offs associated with the feasibility of using adequate sample sizes against the importance of studying some issues regardless of the limited availability of data (cf. Peterson, Smith, & Martorana, 2006, for a discussion of this issue in the context of applied psychology).

An important goal of sampling, then, is to provide an accurate and practical mechanism to enable extrapolation from a sample to a population. The next three chapters present approaches to determining sample size: power analysis, confidence intervals, and computer-intensive methods. Each approach will be described and critiqued in terms of its strengths and limitations. In some ways, the aforementioned strategies for determining sample size can be described as a patchwork quilt of procedures. No single software package exists that allows researchers to determine sample size according to these three strategies across all statistical procedures described in the following chapters. Specific recommendations are provided for each statistical procedure. Readers should be aware that, whenever possible, the approach recommended here is to estimate sample size with GPower, which is a free power analysis program available at http://www.psycho.uniduesseldorf.de/aap/projects/gpower/. For researchers who prefer a comprehensive statistical package, PASS is recommended. PASS is capable of performing a wide range of sample size calculations. Information about PASS can be obtained at http://www.ncss.com/pass_procedures.html. Other options, discussed as appropriate later, include SPSS and SAS scripts and specialized web-based calculators. The appendix provides a more comprehensive discussion of software for sample size determination.

One strategy for determining sample size is statistical power analysis. Power analyses can be performed before collecting data (*a priori*) or after collecting data (*a posteriori*).[1] The following discussion focuses on a priori analysis that seeks to estimate sample size based on acceptable levels of effect size,[2] α, and power. Several authors have suggested a 4:1

ratio of β to α. That is, if the level of α is established a priori at .05, then the corresponding power is $1 - 4(.05) = .80$. This 4:1 ratio of β to α is used in this chapter (cf. Hinkle, Wiersma, & Jurs, 2003).

Methods for estimating statistical power and sample size are well known and have been extensively discussed (e.g., Hoenig & Heisey, 2001; Kraemer & Thiemann, 1987; Lenth, 2001; Murphy & Myors, 2003). Therefore, the purpose of this chapter is to (1) provide a brief description of the rationale and limitations of statistical power analysis and (2) present important issues related to determining sample size for both commonly used and emerging statistical procedures in social work research.

Put simply, statistical power is the probability of detecting an effect. The concept of statistical power is attributed to Neyman and Pearson (1928), although Fisher (1925) addressed similar issues in his discussions of test and design sensitivity (cf. Huberty, 1993 for a detailed discussion). Jacob Cohen is considered by many researchers to be among the most important writers about power analysis. Cohen's work was motivated by his perception that power analysis was largely neglected in psychological research. In a survey of articles published in *Journal of Abnormal and Social Psychology* in the year 1960, Cohen (1962) found the mean power to detect medium effect sizes to be .48. He concluded that the chance of obtaining a significant result was about the same as tossing a head with a fair coin. Hoping to correct for this neglect in statistical power, Cohen published his most popular work, *Statistical Power Analysis for the Behavioral Sciences* (1969/1988).

Following Jacob Cohen's (1962) pioneering work on the power of statistical tests in behavioral research, many authors have stressed the utility of statistical power analysis. Textbooks and articles have appeared that provide tables of power and sample sizes (e.g., Cohen, 1969/1988, 1992, 1994; Cohen & Cohen, 1983; Hager & Möller, 1986; Kraemer & Thiemann, 1987; Lipsey, 1990; Murphy & Myors, 2003; Orme & Hudson, 1995).

An increasing number of computer programs for performing power analysis have become available during the past few years. Power analysis procedures have been incorporated into existing statistical software (e.g., SAS, Stata, S-Plus), and increasing interest in power analysis has resulted in the development of specialized packages (e.g., PASS, GPower, and Power and Precision).[3] In addition, web-based calculators proliferate at a rapid rate. Examples of web-based resources are provided in this and the remaining chapters.

Power is the probability of rejecting the null when a particular alternative hypothesis is true. Power can be defined only in the context of a specific set of parameters, and, accordingly, reference to an alternative hypothesis, expressed as an effect size (discussed subsequently), is necessary. The power of a test, therefore, is defined as $1 - \text{beta}$ (β), where β (or type II error) is the probability of falsely accepting H_0 when H_a is true.[4] Statistical power, then, is the ability of a statistical test to detect an effect if the effect exists (Cohen, 1988). Figure 2.1 depicts an example using a two-tailed test (e.g., a t-test), and a one-tailed alternative, or research hypothesis.

Distribution A (labeled H_0) represents a sampling distribution when the null hypothesis is true (mean or $m = 0$). The portion of the right tail of this distribution labeled $\alpha/2$ contains the means that would result in rejection of H_0. But what if H_0 actually is false?

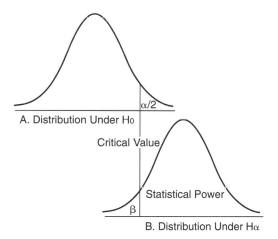

Figure 2.1. Relationships Among Alpha (α), Beta (β), and Power ($1 - \beta$)

Also termed a ***noncentral distribution***,[5] distribution B (labeled H_a) represents one possible sampling distribution when H_0 is false. Even when H_0 is false, some sample values (e.g., means) will fall to the left of the critical region and result in failure to reject a false H_0, and, accordingly, a type II error. The probability of this error is β. When H_0 is false and the test statistic falls to the right of the critical value, H_0 is rejected correctly. The probability of doing this is defined as power $(1 - \beta)$. Conventionally, a test with power greater than .80 (or β is less than or equal to .2) is considered statistically powerful.

Power is a function of the following factors: (1) alpha (α or type I error), (2) beta (β or type II error), (3) magnitude of a hypothesized effect size, (4) the standard deviation of the hypothesized effect size, and (5) sample size. More specifically, power is a function of alpha and beta. As Figure 2.1 illustrates, as α increases, β decreases with a corresponding increase in power. Also, power is a function of effect size (i.e., the true alternative hypothesis, such as an expected difference between groups, how small the effect can be and still be of substantive interest, or the expected size of the effect). As Figure 2.1 illustrates, if the distance between m_0 and m_1 increases, power increases. That is, the chance of finding a difference between the two means depends on the size of the difference; the greater the difference, the more likely it is to be identified, and, consequently, when it is false, H_0 is rejected. Finally, power is a function of N and variance. In general, the variance of the distribution of an effect size decreases as N increases; and, as this variance decreases, power increases.

The logic behind power analysis is compelling: a study should be conducted only if it relies on a sample size that is large enough to provide an adequate and a prespecified probability of finding an effect if an effect exists. If a sample is too small, the study could miss important differences; too large, the study could make unnecessary demands on respondent privacy and time or waste valuable resources. The benefits of power analysis are at least twofold: sample size selection is made on a rational basis rather than using rules of thumb, and the researcher must specify the size of the effect that is substantively interesting.

In power analysis, after specifying (1) an effect size and (2) beta and alpha, an appropriate sample size can be calculated. In general, calculating the power of a planned study involves the following steps:

1. Establish a desired sample size (based on perceived feasibility and other studies).
2. Determine the alpha level (e.g., .05).
3. Calculate beta, assuming the alternative hypothesis is true.
4. Calculate power $(1 - \beta)$.

The computation of statistical power depends on a specific model (or test). The t-test, with its relatively simple formula, can facilitate the discussion of an example that illustrates the calculation of statistical power and the determination of sample size. For example, a social work researcher plans to administer a Satisfaction with Family Life Scale to a random sample of 100 married people, with an equal number of respondents with no children and respondents with at least one child. On this scale, higher scores indicate greater satisfaction. The researcher wants to know whether there is a significant difference in satisfaction with family life between respondents with no children and respondents with at least one child. Specifically, the researcher hypothesizes that respondents with at least one child will have scale scores 6 points higher than respondents with no children. An earlier pilot study $(N = 30)$ from a similar population estimated that Satisfaction with Family Life Scale scores have a standard deviation of 10. Prior to implementation, the researcher decides to determine the statistical power of this study and hopes that power will be .80 or greater.

Her calculations are as follows:

1. α is set at .05.
2. Effect size equals expected difference divided by the standard deviation of scale scores, or $6/10 = .060$.
3. If the null hypothesis is false, then scores will not be distributed around 0 (means are not equal, or the difference between means of

scores will not be 0). That is, if the null hypothesis is false, power is a function of a distribution based on the assumptions of the alternative hypothesis: a distribution with a mean of 6. This shift in the mean of the distribution from 0 to 6 is referred to as the degree of noncentrality, and this noncentrality parameter is termed delta (δ). To determine power, the researcher first must identify beta on this alternative distribution. To identify β on this alternative distribution, compute δ, defined as effect size divided by the square root of the sample size (formula 3.2). Therefore, $\delta = .60$ times the square root of $100/4 = .60$ times $5 = 3.00$.

4. Calculate the proportion of the distribution of values of the alternative hypothesis less than β and subtract this proportion from 1. To calculate this proportion, refer to a (a) cumulative distribution table of noncentral t, (b) table of values under the normal (Z) distribution as an approximation of values of t, or (c) table of power for δ. Tables of power and sample size are available and require no additional computations to estimate power (cf. Howell, 2007, p. 678). Power for a one-tailed test at alpha equals .05 equals .91. A power of .91 means that the researcher would have a 91% chance of rejecting H_0 if it is false. Therefore, based on a desired power of .80, her study is overpowered, and she would consider reducing her sample size. An alternative strategy adopted in subsequent examples is to establish an effect size, set $\alpha = .05$ and $\beta = .80$, and then calculate sample size.

To facilitate the identification of issues and resources related to specific statistical procedures, the following discussion is procedure-specific. As noted earlier, power analyses can be performed before collecting data (a priori) or after collecting data (a posteriori). However, the approach taken here is to focus on a priori analysis that seeks to estimate sample size based on acceptable levels of effect size, $\alpha = .05$, and power or $1 - \beta = .80$. For each statistical test, the following topics are addressed: (1) general issues, including definition of effect size and noncentrality parameter, and (2) recommended approaches.

Differences Between Means

The emphasis here is on hypothesis testing for two or more variables. Readers interested in a detailed discussion of sample size for one sample (single mean) should refer to Howell (2007, chapter 8). In the case of a two-group-mean comparison, the typical effect size index is a standardized mean difference. This index, *d*, was proposed by Jacob Cohen (1962; see Table 1.2 for a summary of commonly used effect sizes). During the 1970s and 1980s, there was discussion about which standard deviation should be used as the denominator in *d*. Two suggestions made were (1) the standard deviation pooled across the two groups proposed by Cohen (1969) and (2) the standard deviation of the control group—the definition of which is not always clear—proposed by Glass (1976). The letter *d* was used by both Cohen and Glass. In practice, the pooled standard deviation, σ_{pooled}, is commonly used (Rosnow & Rosenthal, 1996).

Independent Samples

The *effect size d* is defined as the standardized distance between two means:

$$d = \left[\frac{\mu_1 - \mu_2}{\sigma}\right]$$

Noncentrality parameter:

$$\delta = d\sqrt{\frac{N}{4}} \quad \text{where } N = n_1 + n_2$$

Formula for N desired:

$$N_{desired} = \left(\frac{\delta}{d'}\right)^2$$

Noncentrality parameter for independent-samples t with unequal group sizes:

$$\delta = d\sqrt{\frac{n_h}{2}} = where = n_h = \frac{2n_1 n_2}{n_1 + n_2} \text{ which is the Harmonic mean.}$$

Recommended Approach(es): GPower, PASS

Correlated Samples

When conducting a power analysis for the correlated samples design, the effect of ρ_{12} (correlation between the scores in the one condition and those in the second condition) must be considered by computing d_{Diff}, an adjusted value of the *effect size d:*

$$d_{Diff} = \frac{d}{\sqrt{2(1 - \rho_{12})}}.$$

The denominator of this ratio is the standard deviation of the difference scores rather than the standard deviation of the original scores. The formula for *desired sample size* is:

$$n = \left(\frac{\delta}{d_{Diff}}\right)^2.$$

The *noncentrality parameter* for correlated samples t is defined as:

$$\delta = d\sqrt{N} \quad \text{where } N = \text{number of sample observations}$$

Recommended Approach(es): GPower, PASS; if the sample size is large enough, then there will be little difference between the t distribution and the standard normal curve, and the value of δ can be obtained from a table of power as a function of δ and α (cf. Howell, 2007, p. 678).

Differences Between Proportions

Most frequently, studies compare two or more proportions, but occasionally there is a need to draw statistical inferences about a single proportion. Readers interested in a detailed discussion of sample size for one sample (single proportion) should refer to Fleiss, Levin, and Paik (2003, chapter 2), and Cohen (1988, chapter 5).

Power analysis for tests of proportions can be approached in several ways (cf. Cohen, 1988, chapter 6, for a discussion of alternatives). The ability to detect a difference in magnitude between population proportions (power) is not a simple function of the difference. For example, for fixed sample size and alpha, proportions with equal differences do not have the same power (see Cohen, 1988, for examples). Therefore, Cohen discusses power analysis for proportions in the context of a normal curve test applied to the arcsine transformation of proportions. The arcsine, also termed arcsine root and arcsine square root transformation, converts a binomial distribution to a nearly normal distribution. The effect size h is defined as $\phi_1 - \phi_2$, where P is a proportion and $\Phi = 2$ arcsine $\sqrt{P}$.

Recommended Approach(es): Using h and a predetermined alpha (α), tables are provided in Cohen (1988, chapter 6) to calculate sample size and power. A second option is to consult Fleiss, Levin, and Paik (2003), which provides extensive tables for determining sample size per group for a test of the difference between two proportions (see Table A.4 on pp. 660–682). Using these tables requires the researcher to estimate the size of the two proportions, alpha and beta. The tables provide the equal sample sizes necessary in the two groups for varying values of (1) the hypothesized proportions P_1 and P_2, (2) alpha, and (3) power. A third option is to use the following web-based calculator: http://statpages.org/proppowr.html.

Odds Ratios

An odds ratio is defined as the ratio of the odds of an event occurring in one group to the odds of it occurring in another group. If the probabilities of the event in each of the groups are p (first group) and q (second group), then the odds ratio is:

$$\frac{p/(1-p)}{q/(1-q)} = \frac{p(1-q)}{q(1-p)}.$$

An odds ratio of 1 indicates that the condition or event under study is equally likely in both groups. An odds ratio greater than 1 indicates that the condition or event is more likely in the first group. And an odds ratio less than 1 indicates that the condition or event is less likely in the first group. The odds ratio must be 0 or greater than 0. As the odds of the first group approach 0, the odds ratio approaches 0. As the odds of the second group approach 0, the odds ratio approaches positive infinity.

Let the letters a, b, c, and d represent the frequency counts in a 2×2 table as follows:

a b
c d

Recommended Approach(es): nQuery Advisor. Information about this software can be obtained at http://www.statsol.ie/.

Chi-Square and Contingency Tables (Test of Independence)

Effect size is defined as w. For a 2×2 table, Cohen (1988) defined w as:

$$\phi = \sqrt{\frac{\chi^2}{N}} = w,$$

and for tables 2×3 or larger, w is defined as:

$$\sqrt{\frac{\chi^2}{N(k-1)}}$$

where $k = $ the smaller of the number of rows or the number of columns.

The *noncentrality parameter* is defined as

$$\delta = \left(\frac{2\phi}{\sqrt{1 - \phi^2}} \right) \sqrt{N}.$$

Recommended Approach(es): If contingency table cell counts can be anticipated, the effect size w can be calculated in GPower using the "Calc 'w'" option after "Type of Test: Chi-square Test" is selected. Alternatively, w can be estimated.

ANOVA

Discussion of analysis of variance (ANOVA) is limited to fixed effects models.[6] Calculating power for a random effects model is more complicated (cf. Winer, 1971). A commonly used effect size for ANOVA designs is Cohen's f. Cohen (1988) describes f as an extension of d (discussed earlier). In contrast to d, however, with two or more means, the effect size is not a reflection of the range between means but a quantity similar to a standard deviation. To calculate f, the aforementioned quantity is divided by the standard deviation of the means being compared by ANOVA

$$f = \frac{\sigma_m}{\sigma},$$

where for equal n,

$$\sigma_m = \sqrt{\sum_{i=1}^{k} \frac{(m_i - m)^2}{k}}.$$

To calculate the noncentrality parameter of the F-distribution requires the specification of all of the treatment means and standard deviations.

Moreover, with three or more means, the relationship between their standard deviation and range depends on how the means are dispersed. One simplified specification is the use of mean configuration: a specification of the arrangement of the means (see Cohen, 1988, chapter 8, for an extensive discussion and appropriate tables). Cohen describes three patterns of ways that means can be dispersed over their range: (1) pattern 1 contains one mean at each end and the remaining means at the midpoint; (2) pattern 2 contains means that are equally spaced over the range; and (3) pattern 3 contains means falling at both extremes of the range. When mean configuration is used, the required sample size will not be estimated correctly if the means do not conform to the assumed configuration. To avoid errors, a researcher should consider conducting analyses for several configurations.

Alternatively, effect size d could be specified by the difference between the largest mean and the smallest mean, in units of the within-cell standard deviation (sigma):

$$delta = \frac{\text{largest mean} - \text{smallest mean}}{\text{sigma}}.$$

Although less precise in terms of calculating power, this minimum power specification might be more feasible if there is little empirical experience with a phenomenon. McClelland (1997) has argued that often with fixed effects models more levels of the independent variables are used than needed. That is, using more levels of the independent variable with fixed effects models can weaken the effect across degrees of freedom (e.g., for five levels and four degrees of freedom). Consequently, researchers are more likely to miss detecting a linear effect. The following web page uses the aforementioned minimum specification strategy to perform power analysis for ANOVA designs: http://www.math.yorku.ca/SCS/Online/power/.

This minimum power specification corresponds to the alternative hypothesis that all means other than the two extreme ones are equal to the grand mean. The computations assume: (1) fixed effects and

(2) equal sample sizes in all treatments. Under these assumptions, the *noncentrality parameter* of the *F*-distribution is

$$\delta = N\left(\frac{d^2}{2}\right),$$
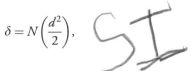

where *N* is the sample size per treatment. As previously, effect-size delta values are typically in the range of 0–3, with values of delta = .25, .75, and 1.25 or greater correspond to "small," "medium," and "large" effects, respectively (Cohen, 1988).

Recommended Approach(es): GPower.

ANCOVA

Analysis of covariance (ANCOVA) is designed to assess group differences on a dependent variable after the effects of one or more covariates are statistically removed. By utilizing the relationship between the covariate and the dependent variable (DV), ANCOVA can increase the power of a treatment effect in a between-subjects design. Adding covariates to an experimental study statistically reduces the error variance and thereby increases the relative effect size. For example, the addition of a covariate with an R^2 of .49 (i.e., a correlation of .7 with the DV) increases power to the same extent as a doubling in sample size; the addition of a covariate with an R^2 of .25 (correlation of .5) increases power to the same extent as an increase in sample size of one third.

However, the inclusion of a covariate introduces additional complexity into power analyses. Taking the strength of relationship between treatment and the covariates into account in a power analysis would be unduly complicated. Fortunately, in a randomized study, the strength of this relationship reflects the vagaries of random assignment, tends to be small, and declines as the sample size increases. As a result, the strength of relationship tends to have a minor influence on the power analysis for randomized studies. For nonrandomized studies, the covariate and the treatment variable tend to be correlated to an extent that cannot be ignored.

In estimating sample size for ANCOVA, the denominator degrees of freedom (df) is adjusted. If k is the number of cells in the design and g is the number of covariates, then groups $= k + g$. In this way the denominator df are reduced because denominator $df = N - (k + g)$. The numerator does not decrease correspondingly and might even increase.

In ANOVA, the *noncentrality parameter* δ is a function of the size of the differences among population treatment means relative to the size of the population within-treatment variance. In ANCOVA, δ is a function of these factors, but it also is a function of the within-treatment population correlation between the covariate and the dependent variables. In addition, δ is affected by the sample relationship between the treatments and the covariate. For a study with two treatments and equal cell frequencies,

$$\delta = \frac{n}{2} \frac{n(u_1 - u_2)^2}{2\sigma^2(1 - p^2)} (1 - r_x^2),$$

where ρ is the within-treatment correlation between the covariate and dependent variable. The quantity r_x is the sample correlation between the covariate and a dummy variable representing the two treatments and measures the sample strength of relationship between the treatments and the covariate.

Recommended Approach(es): GPower.

Repeated-Measures ANOVA

A repeated-measures ANOVA compares a group (within-subjects) across three or more conditions. A typical application is to use a repeated-measures ANOVA to test the equality of a group mean (DV) over time. Note that Cohen (1988) is silent on this issue. GPower and PASS can be used to calculate sample size. A simple alternative approach is to focus the comparison between the pair of means with the smallest expected difference and determine sample size for the correlated t-test (discussed earlier). Calculating the number of cases needed to have an 80% chance of detecting a small effect, $d = .2$, with an estimated correlation between observations of the DV of .27 proceeds as follows:

$$d_{Diff} = \frac{d}{\sqrt{2(1 - \rho_{12})}}, d_{Diff} = \frac{d}{\sqrt{2(1 - \rho_{12})}} = \frac{.2}{\sqrt{2(1 - .27)}} = .166.$$

The approximate sample size needed is

$$n = \left(\frac{2.8}{d_{Diff}}\right)^2 = 285.$$

Recommended Approach(es): GPower.

MANOVA

Multivariate analysis of variance (MANOVA) is a substantially more complicated design than ANOVA, and, therefore, there can be ambiguity about the relationship of each independent with each dependent variable (cf. Muller, LaVange, Ramey, & Ramey, 1992). MANOVA is an ANOVA with several dependent variables. Testing multiple dependent variables is accomplished by creating new dependent variables that maximize group differences. Gain in power obtained from decreased within-group sum of squares might be offset by the loss in these degrees of freedom. One degree of freedom is lost for each dependent variable. See Enders (2003) and Huberty and Morris (1989) for a discussion of issues related to the choice of multiple ANOVAs versus MANOVA.

A widely used measure of *effect size* in MANOVA is Cohen's (1988) f^2. For multiple correlation and regression (MCR), f^2 can easily be expressed as a function of R^2 (the multiple correlation coefficient):

$$f^2 = \frac{R^2}{1 - R^2}.$$

However, in the case of MANOVA, the relationship between f^2 and R^2 is complex. Insight into this relationship between f^2 and R^2 is provided in Tables 10.2.1, 10.2.2, and 10.2.3 in Cohen (1988). A review of these tables can assist researchers who are planning studies and who are familiar with R^2 make decisions with regard to the minimum or expected value of f^2.

Recommended Approach(es): GPower.

MANCOVA

Multiple analysis of covariance (MANCOVA) is similar to MANOVA, but independent variables can be added as "covariates." These covariates serve as control variables for the independent factors, serving to reduce the error term in the model. That is, it is a MANOVA in which the DVs are adjusted for differences in one or more covariates. Resources for estimating sample size for MANCOVA are difficult to identify. One approach is to adapt the aforementioned sample size estimation strategy for MANOVA. That is, use GPower and adjust the denominator *df*. If k is the number of cells in the design and g is the number of covariates, then groups $= k + g$.

Recommended Approach(es): GPower.

Repeated-Measures MANOVA

A repeated-measures MANOVA compares a group (within-subjects) across three or more conditions. A typical application is to use repeated-measures MANOVA to test the equality of two or more group means (DVs) over time. Note that Cohen (1988) is silent on this issue.

Recommended Approach(es): GPower.

Correlation (Pearson's r)

Effect size is defined as

$$d = p_1 - p_0 = p_1 - 0 = p_1,$$

where p_1 is the correlation in the population defined by H_1. That is, r is an effect size. The noncentrality parameter δ is defined as

$$\delta = d\sqrt{n-1} = p_1\sqrt{n-1}.$$

Cohen's (1988) or Howell's (2007) tables can be used to identify the power associated with δ at the established α.

Recommended Approach(es): GPower.

Regression

This effect size is called f^2. First consider the situation in which a researcher wants to calculate the power for a significant R^2. Define $f^2 = R^2/(1 - R^2)$. The noncentrality parameter $= f^2(p + v + 1)$, where $p =$ number of predictor variables and $v = N - p - 1 =$ number of df; alternatively, $f^2 = R^2/(1-R^2)$; therefore, $R^2 = f^2/(1 + f^2)$. Where small, medium, and large effects sizes are as follows:

	f^2	R^2
Small	.02	.02
Medium	.15	.13
Large	.35	.26

Maxwell (2000) raised some interesting questions about the aforementioned use of f^2. According to Maxwell (2000), f^2 addresses a question that is rarely asked. That is, researchers often assume that the overall

R^2 is significant and are more interested in the relative importance or incremental contribution of a predictor. Ultimately, though, the contributions of individual predictors must be placed within the context of the overall model; contributions within the context of a model with a low R^2, no matter how substantial, must be evaluated accordingly. At a minimum, evaluating R^2 seems to be a logical first step and a viable strategy for determining sample size.

Recommended Approach(es): GPower; PASS is a viable alternative for researchers interested in a focus on individual predictors for determining sample size.

Discriminant Function Analysis

Computationally similar to MANOVA, all assumptions for MANOVA apply to discriminant function analysis (DFA). Therefore, sample size can be determined with the aforementioned MANOVA strategies. The principal difference between MANOVA and DFA is the labeling of the dependent and independent variables (Stevens, 2002). Researchers will temporarily need to reconceptualize the DFA model as a MANOVA model by reversing the independent variables (IVs) and the DV. That is, instead of asking: What is the relationship between the IVs and group membership? ask: What characteristics best distinguish groups A and B?

Recommended Approach(es): Reframe as a MANOVA/Hotelling's T-square (two-group case) and use PASS. That is, focus the analysis on the difference between the largest mean and the smallest mean (see chapter 6, example 14, for an illustration of reframing the research question; and see example 1 for an illustration of calculating a confidence interval around a difference between two means).

Logistic Regression

Binomial (or binary) logistic regression is a form of regression that is used when the dependent variable is a dichotomy and the independents are of any type. Multinomial or multiple logistic regression handles dependent variables with more than two classes. When multiple classes of the dependent variable can be ranked, then ordinal logistic regression is preferred to multinomial logistic regression. The following discussion focuses on determining sample size for binary logistic regression. For additional discussion of determining sample size for logistic and Cox regression, see Harrell (1984), Hsieh (1989), and van Belle (2002). For a discussion of sample size determination and ordinal logistic regression, see Walters (2004).

Although assumptions regarding the distribution of predictors are not required for logistic regression, multivariate normality and linearity among the predictors can enhance power, because a linear combination of predictors is used to form the exponent (Tabachnick & Fidell, 2001). When a goodness-of-fit test is used that compares observed with expected frequencies in cells formed by a combination of discrete variables, the analysis may have little power if expected frequencies are too small. It is best if all expected frequencies are greater than 1 and if no more than 20% are less than 5.

Hsieh, Block, and Larsen (1998) evaluated an approach originally introduced by Whittemore (1981). Hsieh et al.'s results suggested that Whittemore's approach not only provides a simple and reasonably accurate method for sample size calculations but also shows that the approach could be expanded to more complex problems. Accordingly, Hsieh et al. (1998) and Vaeth and Skovlund (2004) recommended that the result of a two-sample calculation (e.g., an odds ratio[7]) can be modified by a so-called variance inflation factor such that $N_m = N_1 = (1 - p^2)$ where N_1 and N_m are the required sample sizes with 1 and m covariates, respectively, and p is the multiple correlation coefficient between the covariate of interest and the remaining $m - 1$ covariates.

Recommended Approach(es): PASS and Power and Precision are commercial software options. Alternatively, the following web page computes power, sample size, or minimum detectable odds ratio (OR) for logistic regression with a single binary covariate or two covariates and their interaction: http://www.dartmouth.edu/~eugened/power-samplesize .php. Also, the following web page computes sample size calculations for logistic regression with a continuous exposure variable and an additional continuous covariate or confounding variable: http://biostat.hitchcock.org/MeasurementError/Analytics/SampleSizeCalculationsforLogistic Regression.asp

Cox Regression

Cox regression analyzes data in which the dependent variable is the time-to-event with censoring and covariates. A censored observation is defined as an observation with incomplete information. As discussed earlier, sample size for a simple logistic regression model can be calculated from the formula for a two-sample t-test (Hsieh et al., 1998; Vaeth & Skovlund, 2004). For comparing two treatment groups using a Cox regression model, the sample size can be obtained from the formula for the log-rank test (Hsieh, Lavori, Cohen, & Feussner, 2003). The log-rank test computes a p-value that answers this question: If the two populations have identical survival curves overall, what is the chance that random sampling of subjects would lead to as big a difference in survival (or bigger) as you observed? If the p-value is small ($< .05$), then the null hypothesis that the two populations have identical survival characteristics is rejected (Cox & Oakes, 2001). After calculating the sample size required for a univariate analysis, inflate the sample size as described for logistic regression.

Recommended Approach(es): use nQuery Advisor to calculate the log-rank test of survival in two groups, and use the VIF as described earlier for logistic regression.

Structural Equation Modeling and Confirmatory Factor Analysis

Structural equation modeling (SEM), also termed *analysis of covariance structures,* refers to a hybrid model that integrates path analysis and factor analysis. SEM is used when data consist of multiple indicators for each variable (called latent variables or factors) and specified paths connecting the latent variables. See Tabachnick and Fidell (2001) for an introduction.

Thinking of SEM as a combination of factor analysis and path analysis ensures consideration of SEM's two primary components: the measurement model and the structural model. The measurement model describes the relationships between observed variables and the construct or constructs those variables are hypothesized to measure. The structural model describes interrelationships among constructs. When the measurement model and the structural model are considered together, the model is termed the *composite* or *full structural* model.

In SEM, statistical power is the ability to detect and reject a poor model. In contrast to traditional hypothesis testing, the goal in SEM analysis is to produce a nonsignificant result (i.e., to fail to reject the null of no difference between the proposed and the perfect model). The null hypothesis is assessed by forming a discrepancy function between the proposed model (specified by the researcher) and the perfect or saturated model (one with no constraints that will always fit any data perfectly). Various discrepancy functions can be formed depending on the particular minimization algorithm being used (e.g., maximum likelihood), but the goal remains the same: to derive a test statistic that has a known distribution, and then compare the obtained value of the test statistic against tabled values in order to make a decision about the null hypothesis. Because in SEM the researcher is attempting to develop a theoretical model that accounts for all the covariances among the measured items, a nonsignificant difference between the proposed model and the saturated model is argued to be suggestive of support for the proposed model.

There are at least two approaches to assessing the power of an SEM model. One approach, presented by Satorra and Saris (1985), is as follows:

1. Take the focal model and develop an alternative model by adding an additional parameter (e.g., a standardized path of .2 between two latent variables).

2. Compute the implied covariance matrix based on this alternative model.

3. Submit this covariance matrix to the focal model (which does not specify the existence of this additional parameter) to obtain the chi-square statistic (which now represents a non-centrality parameter).

4. Use this chi-square value and a given alpha level (typically .05) to calculate the power.

This procedure requires the researcher to identify various alternative models. This approach is automated within the SEM program *Mx* (Neale, Boker, Xie, & Maes, 1999), which is available as a free download from http://www.vcu.edu/mx/.

A second, and perhaps more popular, approach, offered by Mac-Callum, Browne, and Sugawara (1996), does not require an alternative model. Instead, it uses the root mean square error of approximation to calculate power (RMSEA[8]; Browne & Cudeck, 1993; Hu & Bentler, 1999; Steiger, 1990). This index weighs absolute fit, which declines whenever a parameter is removed from the model, against model complexity, such that the benefits of parsimony are considered along with fit (Steiger, 1990). Models fitting with RMSEA <.05 are usually considered to be "close" fits; those between .05 and .08 are "fair" fits, between .08 and .10 are "mediocre" fits, and above .10 are "poor" fits (MacCallum et al., 1996). Change in model fit from one proposed model to another is assessed by $\chi^2/\Delta df$ and by the 95% confidence interval (CI) of ε_a generated by this change. MacCallum et al. (1996) suggested that a CI be calculated that should include values between 0 and .05 to indicate the possibility of good fit.

MacCallum et al. (1996) provide both tables and an SAS routine for calculating power and minimum sample size. The SAS routine is available for download from http://www.math.yorku.ca/SCS/sasmac/csm power.html. NIESEM is a DOS-based program for calculating point and interval estimates of noncentrality-based fit statistics used in structural equation modeling. NIESEM also performs power analysis according to the methods of MacCallum et al. (1996). The program is available as a free download from http://rubens.its.unimelb.edu.au/~dudgeon/.

Recommended Approach(es): NIESEM.

Multilevel Analysis

Research that seeks to describe data observed at distinct hierarchical levels is termed *multilevel analysis, research,* or *modeling.* For an overview of multilevel models, see, for example, Klein and Kozlowski (2000). For caveats regarding multilevel models, see Kreft (1996) and Hox (2002). Stratification and clustering are commonly used sampling strategies in multilevel analysis. However, cluster and stratified samples typically have sampling errors much larger than simple random samples (SRS) of the same size. The reason is that elements in a cluster or strata are likely to be more homogeneous because of (1) selective grouping effects (e.g., people move into a neighborhood of similar people), (2) exposure to common environments or influences, (3) the effects of interacting with others in the cluster, or (4) some combination of these factors (Henry, 1990). Consequently, a sample of size N, drawn using SRS from a population, will usually be more efficient (i.e., have smaller sampling errors) than a sample of the same size drawn from clusters or strata. A way to quantify design efficiency is to calculate design effect, which is the ratio of the sampling variance in the sampling method actually used to the sampling variance if SRS were used (Kish, 1965).

Two main components of the design effect are the intraclass correlation and the cluster sample size. The intraclass correlation is the degree of homogeneity of people within clusters (Kish, 1965). When the intraclass correlation is larger, the design effect is larger. The amount that the sample size needs to be adjusted is directly related to the design effect. For example, a design effect of 3 means that the sample size needs to be three times as large as it would be using SRS. Alternatively, the design effect can be understood as relating to the sampling variance. In general, what is at issue is how much standard errors are underestimated in stratified and cluster samples compared with SRS (Kish, 1965). That is, a design effect of 3 means that sampling variance is three times as large as it would be in SRS. The design effect is difficult to calculate before surveys are conducted, so usually estimates are used. For well-designed studies, with both stratification and clustering, the design effect ranges from 1 to 3, but higher values, up to 10, are not uncommon

(Lê & Verma, 1997; Henry, 1990). When cluster sampling is part of the design, a reasonable approach is to use a design effect of 2 or 3.

Although few in number, simulation studies suggest that group-level sample size is generally more important than total sample size, with large individual-level samples partially compensating for a small number of groups; that is, a large number of groups is more important than a large number of individuals per group. A typical approach to estimating sample size for multilevel analysis begins by determining power for an SRS. Next, adjustments are made for the differences between the SRS and the planned multilevel design (i.e., the design effect).

Many of the advantages of multilevel models over traditional methods come at the expense of greater model complexity. More complicated models may be closer to reality, but testing model fit and examination of model assumptions is more difficult. If the model is true, multilevel estimates are less biased and more efficient than those obtained using other methods; however, models are less parsimonious and need larger data sets, and estimation becomes complicated. Sample size and power calculations for multilevel hypothesis testing are particularly complex. Power, for example, depends both on the number of groups and on the number of individuals per group. The centering of explanatory variables also raises more complicated issues than it does in traditional regression models, as does the estimation of variance explained at different levels and by different variables, particularly for models with many random coefficients and for nonlinear models. Several authors have warned against the rapid incorporation of complex multilevel models before their performance is adequately understood and evaluated, and especially when it is done with little regard to the adequacy of the data and the inferences that can be drawn from it (Hox, 2002; Kreft, 1996).

Recommended Approach(es): PINT is a program for determining standard errors and optimal sample sizes in multilevel designs with two levels. The program calculates approximate standard errors for estimates of fixed effect parameters in hierarchical linear models with two levels. For interested readers, the formulas are derived in Snijders and Bosker (1993). The program can be downloaded from http://stat.

gamma.rug.nl/Pint_211.zip. Optimal Design Software (OD) is another program for power analysis available as a free download from http://sitemaker.umich.edu/group-based/files/od156.zip. A manual for OD is available from the author's web page: http://www-personal.umich.edu/~rauden/.

In summary, this chapter has (1) provided a brief description of the rationale and limitations of statistical power analysis and (2) presented important issues related to determining sample size for both commonly used and emerging statistical procedures in social work research. In the next chapter, a second strategy for determining sample size—confidence intervals—is discussed.

3

Confidence Intervals

Measures of Precision

A second strategy is to determine sample size based on the width of a desired confidence interval (CI). The CI was introduced by Jerzey Neyman and developed further with Egon Pearson. A CI is a range of values around which a population parameter (e.g., true mean) is likely to lie in the long run (Neyman, 1952). For example, assuming a normal distribution, if samples of the same size are drawn repeatedly from a population and a 95% CI is calculated around each sample's mean (i.e., plus or minus two standard errors from the mean), then 95% of these intervals should contain the population mean.

A second interpretation of a CI is as a significance test (Schmidt & Hunter, 1997). For example, if the value of 0 falls within an interval, the estimate is not statistically significant at the level of $1 -$ the CI.

CIs can be classified as central or noncentral (Smithson, 2003). *Central CIs* are probably more familiar to researchers and are estimates of the precision of parameters such as means. *Noncentral CI* sare measures of the precision of standardized effect sizes such as Cohen's *d*. Noncentral CIs are not computed in the same manner as CIs for statistics such as means or standard deviations (*SD*s). CIs for sample statistics, such as means and *SD*s, can be computed using formulas, and these computations have been incorporated in commonly used statistical programs for several decades. Constructing CIs around effect sizes, on the other hand, raises two somewhat daunting technical difficulties. First, noncentral t- and F-distributions, with which many researchers are unfamiliar, must be used to construct these effect-size intervals (Fleishman, 1980; Steiger & Fouladi, 1992); these are not the central t- and F-distributions taught in most contemporary doctoral programs or statistics textbooks. Second, a generic formula cannot be employed to compute CIs for effect sizes. Instead, computer estimation must be used. Commonly available software (e.g., SPSS, SAS) can be programmed to provide these "iterative" estimates (Bird, 2002; Smithson, 2001).

Iterative estimation is also necessary in various other statistical procedures with which many researchers might be more familiar, such as the estimation of communalities and rotations in factor analysis. A brief comment on the iterative use of noncentral distributions in building CIs around d is warranted, although this process is extremely technical and although considerably more detail is available elsewhere (e.g., Cumming & Finch, 2001; Smithson, 2001). Because a formula cannot be used for this process, one tail of the effect-size CI is iteratively estimated at a time. For example, for the left tail, and assuming a 95% interval is being constructed, a function of the noncentral distribution called the noncentrality parameter is estimated, and the percentage of the area under this curve that is immediately to the right of the d value or a function of this value is computed. The noncentrality parameter is iteratively tweaked until $1/2$ (e.g., $.05/2 = .025$) of the area in the noncentral distribution is to the right of the d value or a function of this value. Then, for example, the mean of this noncentral distribution is found, and that value defines the left boundary of the CI for d. The process is then repeated to iteratively estimate the right CI boundary. The two boundaries can be found either left first or right first, because the boundaries are estimated independently using two different noncentral distributions with different noncentrality parameters.

It is important to emphasize that CIs around parameters such as means and effect sizes are not the same entities, even though the data and sample size are the same for both computations. This is illustrated by the fact that the widths or precisions of the intervals usually differ. That is, the width of noncentral CIs (e.g., for Cohen's d) is usually larger than the width of central CIs (e.g., for a mean). See chapter 6, example 19, for an example of calculating a CI for an effect size.

Proponents of CIs emphasize that CIs can provide information about an estimate's precision. That is, the width of a CI indicates precision (i.e., the degree of random error associated with it), which is determined by the chosen level of confidence. A narrow CI implies high precision: plausible values can be specified within a narrow range. A wide interval implies poor precision: plausible values can be specified only within a broad range. A wide CI possibly is an indication of inadequate sample size. Therefore, choosing a 99% CI rather than a 95% CI will increase the accuracy of the CI (i.e., it will have a greater chance of including the population parameter) but will decrease its precision (i.e., it will be wider than the corresponding 95% CI).

CIs can be estimated before conducting a study and the width can be used to guide the choice of sample size. A CI can be computed even if no null is stated. After a study, proponents argue, CIs can provide information about precision that might be more useful and accessible than a statistical power value. Proponents also argue that because CIs combine information on location and precision, they can often be used to infer significance levels.

The use of CIs is not a panacea. Although CIs around, for example, a difference can be a useful tool for examining the magnitude of the difference, CIs around effect sizes and strength of association measures are relatively large and appear to be less useful (Barnette, 2005). Although not unique to CIs, there is a temptation to interpret the long-run coverage rate as if it applies to each individual CI. It should be emphasized that the confidence level is based on repeated sampling (such as the construction of many intervals by members of a research class) but that for a given case there usually will be a single interval under consideration. This single CI is either correct or incorrect (all or nothing), but the confidence level gives us an indication of the proportion of correct intervals that can be expected when repeating the estimation procedure. Unresolved problems include establishing meaningful guidelines for confidence levels and acceptable interval widths.

Another issue that confronts any researcher using CIs around effect sizes is the question of what is a noteworthy effect. There is no definitive answer to this question. Smithson (2001) suggests, as a beginning point, that researchers could rely on Cohen's (1988) benchmarks. For example, for R^2, .01 = small, .09 = medium, and .25 = large. Consequently, when R^2 = .05, the lower limit of the 95% CI should exceed .09, which is comparable to the ability to distinguish a large from a medium effect. In addition, when R^2 = .10, the upper limit of the 95% CI should fall below .25, and the lower limit should exceed .01. It should be noted that Cohen had reservations about his proposed, tentative benchmarks of what might be "small," "medium," and "large" effects (Kirk, 1996; Thompson, 2002).

Cohen's diffidence toward criteria for characterizing effect sizes was, in part, a consequence of his opinion that the size of an effect depends on what is being studied. On the one hand, small but replicable effects for very important outcomes might be noteworthy. On the other hand, extremely large effects might be needed for results to be noteworthy for relatively unimportant outcomes. Finally, for many small but realistic data sets, the 95% CI often can seem disappointingly wide (Frick, 1995). That is, for small data sets, CIs are often very broad and hence allow inexact estimates.

There is growing support for the use of CI estimation either to supplement or substitute for hypothesis testing. In social work, Orme and Hudson (1995) have described the use of CIs as an approach to estimating sample size and have compared the CI results method with those obtained from statistical power analysis. These authors suggest that the CI method provides sample size guidelines that can result in precise estimates and powerful tests for nontrivial effect sizes. There are formulas and tables for determining sample size that are based on desired CI widths, rather than desired power and hypothesized effect size (e.g., Darlington, 1990; Kupper & Hafner, 1989).

The purpose of this chapter is to (1) provide a brief description of the rationale and limitations of CIs and (2) present important issues related to calculating CIs for both commonly used and emerging statistical procedures in social work research. The emphasis is on conceptual rather than statistical description, although more statistically intensive supplemental readings will be identified. For each statistical procedure discussed in this chapter, recommended approaches to estimating central CIs and, when appropriate, noncentral CIs are presented.

According to Borenstein (1994), there are six steps to constructing a CI. These steps are as follows:

1. Select a confidence level. The confidence level refers to the likelihood that the true population parameter is within the range specified by the CI. The confidence level is usually expressed as a percentage. Therefore, a 95% confidence level suggests that the probability that the true population parameter is within the CI is .95.

2. Compute alpha. Alpha refers to the likelihood that the true population parameter is outside the CI. Alpha is usually expressed as a proportion. Therefore, if the confidence level is 95%, then alpha would equal $1 - .95$, or .05.

3. Identify a sample statistic (e.g., mean, SD) to serve as a point estimate of the population parameter.

4. Specify the sampling distribution of the statistic. Suppose that we draw all possible samples of size n from a given population. Suppose further that we compute a statistic (e.g., a mean, proportion, SD) for each sample. The probability distribution of this statistic is called a sampling distribution.

5. Based on the sampling distribution of the statistic, find the value for which the cumulative probability is $1 - $ alpha/2. That value is the upper limit of the CI. A cumulative probability refers to the probability that the value falls within a specified range. Frequently, cumulative probabilities refer to the probability that a random variable is less than or equal to a specified value.

6. In a similar way, find the value for which the cumulative probability is alpha/2. That value is the lower limit of the CI.

Difference Between Two Means

The standard error of the estimated difference is defined as

$$\sqrt{\frac{\sigma_1^2}{n_1} + \frac{\sigma_2^2}{n_2}},$$

where the subscripts 1 and 2 indicate whether the values come from the first or the second group. According to this formula, the standard error and, consequently, the width of the CI narrow as sample size increases. When planning a study comparing two groups, researchers might consider using different sample sizes for each. That is, if one group is much more variable than the other group, using a larger sample size in the group with the larger variance might be more feasible than trying to get equal numbers in each group.

Recommended Approach(es) for Central CIs: (1) Use nQuery. (2) To obtain a 95% CI, multiply the standard error of the mean (SEm) by 1.96 and then add it to and subtract it from the mean. This will give you a lower limit and an upper limit; that is, CI(95%) = Mean + (1.96) (SEm). To obtain a 99% CI, just multiply the SEm by 2.58, and then add it to and subtract it from the mean; that is, CI(99%) = Mean ± (2.58) (SEm). (3) The following calculator computes CIs of a sum, difference, quotient, or product of two means, assuming both groups follow a Gaussian distribution: http://graphpad.com/quickcalcs/ErrorProp1.cfm. (4) The following Excel file calculates CIs: http://www.pedro.fhs.usyd.edu .au/Utilities/CIcalculator.xls.

Confidence Intervals for Standardized Effect Sizes

What if, instead of a CI around the difference between two means, a researcher is interested in the CI around the effect size d? In this case, the researcher must calculate the CI around d rather than the difference between two means. As discussedearlier, the appropriate probability distribution is for noncentral values of t; that is, values of t if the null hypothesis of no difference between the means is false. Calculations of CIs for the noncentral t distribution are considerably more complicated than the calculation of CIs for the more familiar central t distribution. In the case of the central t distribution, there are numerous tables and programs to find points on this distribution. In the case of the noncentral t distribution, there are an infinite number of such distributions, one for every possible value of the parameter (i.e., effect size), making tables of little value.

Recommended Approach(es) for Noncentral CIs: Michael Smithson has provided macros for use with SPSS and SAS. These macros, with documentation, can be used to calculate CIs for noncentral t-, F-, and chi-square distributions and can be downloaded from http://www .anu.edu.au/psychology/people/smithson/details/CIstuff/CI.html. (See chapter 6, example 19.) Alternatively, interested readers can download a macro for calculating CIs for d, with instructions, from http://core .ecu.edu/psyc/wuenschk/SPSS/CI-d-SPSS.zip. This macro requires the user to specify the sample sizes and the values of t and df. Using the pooled variances, values of t and degrees of freedom are recommended. A third option for calculating CIs for the noncentral t-distribution is Effect Size Calculator, which is a Microsoft Excel spreadsheet. This spreadsheet will calculate the effect size d for the difference between two means and plot the difference and its CI on a graph. It will also calculate a t-test to determine whether the difference is statistically significant. The spreadsheet can be downloaded from http://www .cemcentre.org/renderpage.asp?linkID=30325017.

Difference Between Two Proportions

1. Compute $p_1 - p_2$.
2. Find z for CI using a table of z-values. An online table is located at http://davidmlane.com/hyperstat/z_table.html.
3. Estimate $\sigma_{p_1 - p_2}$ with the formula:

$$s_{p_1 - p_2} = \sqrt{\frac{p_1(1-p_1)}{n_1} + \frac{p_2(1-p_2)}{n_2}},$$

where p_1 and p_2 are the proportions and n_1 and n_2 are the respective group sizes.

Recommended Approach(es): (1) The following web page calculates the CI for the difference between two independent proportions: http://faculty.vassar.edu/lowry/prop2_ind.html. (2) WhatIS is an expression evaluator (with registers for constants, interim results, and formulas) and calculator for probability values (and their inverse), CIs, and time spans. The program can be downloaded from http://www.sph.emory.edu/~cdckms/WinPepi/WHATIS.EXE.

Odds Ratios

Let the letters a, b, c, and d represent the frequency counts in a 2×2 table as follows:

a b
c d

Then the odds ratio would be ad/bc (see chapter 2 for a more extensive description). The odds ratio is skewed, so we cannot easily compute a standard error for the odds ratio itself. We can, however, find a standard error for the natural logarithm of the odds ratio. It is simply

$$\sqrt{\frac{1}{a} + \frac{1}{b} + \frac{1}{c} + \frac{1}{d}}.$$

As any of the counts in the 2×2 table increase, the CI for the log odds ratio shrinks. Also, the smallest count in the 2×2 table plays the largest role in determining the size of the standard error.

Recommended Approach(es): Calculator for CIs of odds ratio: http://www.hutchon.net/ConfidORselect.htm.

Chi-Square and Contingency Tables (Test of Independence)

Recommended Approach(es) for Central CIs: Given a chi-square statistic, this script identifies whether it falls into a selected confidence range: http://www.hostsrv.com/webmaa/app1/MSP/webm1010/chi2.

Recommended Approach(es) for Noncentral CIs: For noncentral chi-square, see Michael Smithson's macro for use with SPSS and SAS. This macro, with documentation, can be used to calculate CIs for noncentral chi-square distributions, and it can be downloaded from http://www.anu.edu.au/psychology/people/smithson/details/CIstuff/CI.html.

ANOVA

Discussion of ANOVA is limited to fixed effects models. Calculating CIs for a random effects model is more complicated (cf. Fidler & Thompson, 2001).

One strategy is to focus on the desired magnitude of R^2. Although it is not used frequently, an R^2 can be calculated for an ANOVA model. The R^2 represents how well all the levels of the grouping (nominal) variable fit the data. As discussed in chapter 2, with three or more levels for the nominal variable, questions about the differences between pairs or combinations of means can be asked.

A second strategy is to compare means through the use of simple contrasts. Contrast coding creates a new variable by assigning numeric weights to the levels of an ANOVA factor under the constraint that the sum of the weights equals 0. Simple contrasts include the case of the difference between two factor means, such as $\mu_1 - \mu_2$. If one wishes to compare treatments 1 and 2 with treatment 3, one way of expressing this is by: $\mu_1 + \mu_2 - 2(\mu_3)$. Note that $\mu_1 - \mu_2$ has coefficients $+1$, -1, that $\mu_1 + \mu_2 - 2(\mu_3)$ has coefficients $+1$, $+1$, -2, and that these coefficients sum to 0.

Because the calculation of CIs for a contrast is mathematically complex, readers are encouraged to use software for these computations. Interested readers should refer to the following web page for a detailed discussion of contrasts and the calculation of CIs for contrasts: http://www.itl.nist.gov/div898/handbook/prc/section4/prc426.htm.

A third strategy is to focus on a minimum power specification. Determining the sample size for an ANOVA design is usually difficult because of the need to specify all of the treatment means and standard deviations, so an alternative is to focus on the difference between the largest mean and the smallest mean. Although less precise in terms of determining sample size, this minimum power specification might be more feasible if there is little empirical experience with a phenomenon. Moreover, this minimum power specification corresponds to the alternative hypothesis that all means other than the two extreme ones are equal to the grand mean. In this way, the problem is reduced to calculating a CI for the difference between two means (discussed earlier).

Recommended Approach(es) for Central CIs: Statistica and nQuery compute CIs for one-way ANOVAs and around contrasts.

Confidence Intervals for Standardized Effect Sizes

Measures of effect size in ANOVA can be thought of as the correlation between an effect and the dependent variable. If the value of the measure of association is squared, it can be interpreted as the proportion of variance in the dependent variable that is attributable to the effect. Two commonly used measures of effect size in ANOVA are eta squared (η^2) and partial eta squared (η_p^2). Eta squared and partial eta squared are estimates of the degree of association for the sample.

Eta squared is analogous to r^2. Therefore, an $\eta^2 = .367$ means that 36.7% of the variability in the dependent variable can be explained or accounted for by the independent variable. It is calculated as

$$\eta^2 = \frac{t^2}{t^2 + df}.$$

Eta squared is the proportion of the total variance that is attributed to an effect. Alternatively, it is calculated as the ratio of the effect variance (SS_{effect}) to the total variance (SS_{total}), or

$$\eta^2 = SS_{effect}/SS_{total}.$$

The partial eta squared is the proportion of the the effect + error variance that is attributable to the effect. The formula differs from the eta-squared formula in that the denominator includes the SS_{effect} plus the SS_{error} rather than the SS_{total}, or

$$\eta_{p^2} = SS_{effect}/(SS_{effect} + SS_{error}).$$

Recommended Approach(es) for Noncentral CIs: Smithson's SPSS and SAS macros for CIs around partial eta squared (noncentral F-distribution) can be downloaded from http://www.anu.edu.au/psychology/people/smithson/details/CIstuff/CI.html

ANCOVA

As discussed in chapter 2, utilizing the relationship between a covariate and the dependent variable reduces error variance. However, the inclusion of a covariate introduces additional complexity into calculating CIs around contrasts. Fortunately, in a randomized study, the strength of this relationship reflects the vagaries of random assignment, tends to be small, and declines as the sample size increases. For nonrandomized studies the covariate and the treatment variable tend to be correlated to an extent that cannot be ignored.

Recommended Approach(es): One strategy is to compute the CI for a contrast as described previously for an ANOVA model and consider this CI as a conservative estimate of the true CI of the ANCOVA.

Repeated-Measures ANOVA

Recommended Approach(es): As for ANCOVA, a simple alternative approach is to focus on the difference between the largest mean and the smallest mean and calculate a CI around this mean difference.

MANOVA/MANCOVA/Repeated-Measures MANOVA

As discussed in chapter 2, MANOVA is a substantially more complicated design than ANOVA, and, therefore, there can be ambiguity about the relationship of each independent with each dependent variable. Testing the multiple dependent variables is accomplished by creating new dependent variables that maximize group differences. One strategy is to select a one-way model, focus on the difference between the largest mean and the smallest mean, and calculate a CI around this mean difference.

Recommended Approach(es): Statistica produces exact standardized CIs for individual (nonsimultaneous) planned contrasts (http://www .statsoft.com/quote/order.html#power). The PSY program constructs individual CIs on planned contrasts, simultaneous CIs for planned or post hoc analyses of single-factor between-subjects and within-subjects designs, and two-factor designs with one between-subjects and one within-subjects factor. PSY can be downloaded from http://www.psy .unsw.edu.au/research/psy.htm.

Correlation

Recommended Approach(es): For the CI around *r*, see the web page http://faculty.vassar.edu/lowry/rho.html.

Multiple Regression

When calculating a regression line, one estimates the mean of the population of *Y* at any value of *X*. Thus the regression line represents the mean $\hat{Y}_i$ at any value of the independent variable X. This estimated mean is normally distributed, and one may ask the question about the CI of the estimated Y. It can be shown that the ratio $(\hat{Y} - \mu_y)/s_2$ follows a t-distribution with $n - 2$ degrees of freedom. From this, one can calculate the CI of the estimated Y by the following equation:

$$s_3^2 = s_{y,x}^2 \left[1 + \frac{1}{n} + \frac{(x - \bar{x})^2}{[x^2]} \right],$$

with

$$s_{y,x}^2 = \sum \frac{(Y_i - \hat{Y}_i)^2}{n - 2},$$

$$[x^2] = \sum_i (x_i - \bar{x})^2$$

The variance σ^2 may be estimated by

$$s^2 = \frac{\sum e_i^2}{n - 2},$$

also known as the mean square error (or MSE). The estimate of the standard error s is the square root of the MSE.

MSE is the sum of the squares (SS) of the difference between the desired response and the actual system output (the error).

Mean square error (MSE) =

$$MSE = \frac{\sum (Y_i - \hat{Y}_i)^2}{n - p}$$

Mean square regression (MSR) =

$$MSR = \frac{\sum (\hat{Y}_i - \bar{Y})^2}{p - 1}$$

Alternatively, use R or R^2 as an effect size, and calculate the noncentral CI around this measure.

Recommended Approach(es): To calculate the CI interval of a regression coefficient, visit http://www.danielsoper.com/statcalc/calc26 .aspx. For the CI around R^2 or R, the following options are available: (1) The following calculator will compute the 99%, 95%, and 90% CIs for a squared multiple correlation (i.e., an R^2) given the value of the squared multiple correlation, the number of predictors in the model, and the total sample size: http://www.danielsoper.com/statcalc/calc28.aspx. (2) The following calculator will compute an adjusted R^2 value (i.e., the population squared multiple correlation), given a sample R^2, the number of predictors in the model, and the total sample size: http://www .danielsoper.com/statcalc/calc25.aspx. (3) $R2$ is a free program that calculates CIs around multiple R-square. The program can downloaded from http://www.interchg.ubc.ca/steiger/r2.zip, and the manual can be downloaded from http://www.interchg.ubc.ca/steiger/r2.pdf. (4) Smithson's macros for SPSS and SAS can be downloaded from http://www .anu.edu.au/psychology/people/smithson/details/CIstuff/CI.html.

Discriminant Function Analysis (DFA)

Computationally similar to MANOVA, all assumptions for MANOVA apply to DFA. Therefore, sample size can be determined with the aforementioned MANOVA strategies. The principal difference between MANOVA and DFA is the labeling of the dependent and independent variables (Stevens, 2002). Researchers will, at least temporarily, need to reconceptualize the DFA model as a MANOVA model (i.e., reverse the IVs and the DV). That is, instead of asking, What characteristics best distinguish A and B group membership? ask, What is the relationship between the IVs and group membership?

Recommended Approach(es): Reframe the research question as a MANOVA/Hotelling's T-square (two-group case) and use the minimum power specification presented for ANOVA. That is, focus the analysis on the CI around the difference between the largest mean and the smallest mean. (See chapter 6, example 14, for an illustration of reframing the research question; and see example 1 for an illustration of calculating a CI around a difference between two means.)

Logistic Regression

The CI around the logistic regression coefficient is plus or minus 1.96 × ASE, where ASE is the asymptotic standard error of logistic b. "Asymptotic" in ASE means the smallest possible value for the standard error when the data fit the model. It also represents the highest possible precision. The real (enlarged) standard error is typically slightly larger than ASE. Typically, the real ASE is used if it is hypothesized that noise in the data are systematic; the ASE is used if it is hypothesized that noise in the data are random.

Logit coefficients (logits), also called unstandardized logistic regression coefficients or effect coefficients or simply "parameter estimates" in SPSS output, correspond to b coefficients in ordinary least squares (OLS) regression. Both can be used to construct prediction equations and generate predicted values, which in logistic regression are called logistic scores. The SPSS table which lists the b coefficients also lists the standard error of b, the Wald statistic and its significance, and the odds ratio (labeled Exp(b)), as well as confidence limits on the odds ratio.

Recommended Approah(es): No practical strategies have emerged in the literature.

Cox Regression

Relative risk (RR) is used frequently in the statistical analysis of binary outcomes in which the outcome of interest has a low probability of occurring. Therefore, RR often is used to compare the risk of developing a disease in people receiving a new medical treatment versus people receiving an established (standard of care) treatment or a placebo.

In a simple comparison between an experimental group and a control group, an RR of 1 means that there is no difference in risk between the two groups. An RR of <1 means that the event is less likely to occur in the experimental group than in the control group. An RR of >1 means that the event is more likely to occur in the experimental group than in the control group.

The log of RR is usually taken to have an approximately normal sampling distribution. This permits the construction of a CI that is symmetric around log(RR); that is,

$$CI = \log(RR) \pm SE \times z_\alpha,$$

where $z\alpha$ is the standard score for the chosen level of significance and SE the standard error. The antilog can be taken of the two bounds of the log-CI, giving the high and low bounds for an asymmetric CI around the RR. In regression models, the treatment is typically included as a dummy variable along with other factors that may affect risk. The relative risk is normally reported for the mean of the sample values of the explanatory variables.

Recommended Approach(es): No practical strategies have emerged in the literature.

Structural Equation Modeling and Confirmatory Factor Analysis

As discussed in chapter 2, one popular measure of model fit is root mean square error of approximation (RMSEA). This measure is based on the noncentrality parameter. Good models have an RMSEA of .05 or less. Models whose RMSEA is .10 or more have poor fit. A CI can be computed for this index. First, the value of the noncentrality parameter is determined by $\chi^2 - df$. The CI for noncentrality parameter can be determined for χ^2, df, and the width of the CI. Then these values are substituted for $\chi^2 - df$ into the formula for the RMSEA. Ideally the lower value of the 90% CI includes or is very near 0 and the upper value is not very large, that is, less than .08.

Recommended Approach(es): Use NIESEM, which is a DOS-based program for calculating point and interval estimates of noncentrality-based fit statistics used instructural equation modeling (SEM). NIESEM is free and available for download from http://rubens.its.unimelb.edu .au/~dudgeon/.

Multilevel Analysis

Recommended Approach(es): Use one of the aforementioned approaches and then adjust for sampling strategy, as described in chapter 2.

In summary, this chapter has (1) provided a brief description of the rationale and limitations of CIs, (2) presented important issues related to calculating CIs for both commonly used and emerging statistical procedures in social work research, and (3) identified additional confidence-related resources, including supplemental readings, web-based and personal computer-based power calculators. In the next chapter, a third strategy for determining sample size, computer-intensive methods, is discussed.

4

Computer-Intensive Methods

Basic Concepts

The previous chapters on power analysis and confidence intervals sug
gest that researchers who are searching for a comprehensive approach
to determining sample size are faced with a patchwork quilt of procedures. At a minimum, there is a disparity between the range of ana-
lytical strategies and the number of available approaches to determining
sample size. Formulas range from simple, such as those for means and
proportions, to more complex, such as those to determine sample size
for t-tests, ordinary least squares regression, one-way analysis of variance, two-way contingency tables, and correlation analysis. Approximations exist for other statistical models, such as multivariate analysis
of variance and logistic regression, but the accuracy of these approximations can be difficult to establish. Thus the list of all statistical tests for
which exact sample size calculation methods exist is much smaller than
the list of all statistical tests. When no formula exists, as happens with
more complex statistical designs, the researcher can try to determine
sample size for a simplified version of the study design and then extrap-
olate this sample size to the planned, and more complex, study design. In addition, no single software package can be used to determine

sample size across all commonly used analysis strategies, and many researchers will need several software packages, some of which can be quite costly.

For statistical models without appropriate formulas, another approach to determining sample size is the use of computer-intensive strategies (CISs; Efron, 1979). CISs in statistics, also termed resampling strategies, have been available since the 1950s (Tukey, 1991). The term *computer-intensive strategies* describes a range of approaches, including bootstrapping and Monte Carlo methods (see Efron, 1982, for a comprehensive overview). CISs rely on the use of random sampling techniques and computer simulation to obtain approximate solutions to mathematical or physical problems. The emphasis in this chapter is on an adaptation of bootstrapping and Monte Carlo methods to determine sample size.

The Bootstrap

According to Efron (1982), the term **bootstrap**, derived from the old saying about pulling yourself up by your own bootstraps, is based on the idea that the one available sample gives rise to all the others. Proponents argue that this computationally intensive approach provides freedom from two limiting factors that dominate traditional statistical theory: (1) the assumption that the data conform to a bell-shaped curve, called the normal distribution; and (2) the need to focus on statistical measures whose theoretical properties can be analyzed mathematically.

In bootstrapping, the original data set is sampled randomly, but with replacement, to produce "new" data sets (Good, 1999). To bootstrap, first assume that the population is distributed exactly as an obtained sample. Second, construct a population (sometimes termed a **pseudo-population**) that exactly mirrors the shape of the obtained sample. Third, draw samples of a given size from this pseudo-population with replacement. That is, each sample consists of the same number of elements, but not necessarily the same elements. Replacement is crucial because, otherwise, resampling would create the same sample multiple times. Fourth, perform the planned analysis on each sample. And fifth, average the results over all samples drawn from the pseudo-population.

Monte Carlo Methods

The expression *Monte Carlo (MC) method* describes a group of stochastic techniques; that is, MC methods are based on the use of random numbers and probability statistics to investigate problems. In mathematics, a stochastic process is a random function. MC methods are used to solve a range of problems, from economics to nuclear physics to regulating the flow of traffic. Strictly speaking, to call something a "Monte Carlo" experiment, all that is needed is the use of random numbers to explore a problem. The use of MC methods to model physical problems, for example, allows researchers to examine more complex systems that otherwise would be more difficult. Solving equations that describe the interactions between two atoms is fairly simple; solving the same equations for hundreds or thousands of atoms is impossible. With MC methods, a large system can be sampled in a number of random configurations, and those data can be used to describe the system as a whole.

Random Number Generator

As discussed, in both bootstrapping and Monte Carlo procedures, a statistic of interest is calculated from multiple samples. Bootstrapping selects from the populations of observed cases, sampling *with* replacement. MC typically samples with replacement from theoretical distributions with specific characteristics. It might seem like a daunting task to use the characteristics of a single sample to construct an infinitely large population and then to draw multiple random samples from this population. But, with the help of a computer, it is a relatively simple process, because most comprehensive statistics packages (e.g., SPSS, SAS) include a random number generator. A random number generator produces numbers chosen as if by chance from some specified distribution such that selection of a large set of these numbers reproduces the underlying distribution. Almost always, such numbers are also required to be independent, so that there are no correlations between successive numbers. Computer-generated random numbers are sometimes called *pseudo-random* numbers, whereas the term *random* is reserved for the output of unpredictable physical processes. When used without qualification, the word *random* usually means "random with a uniform distribution." A uniform distribution, sometimes also known as a rectangular distribution, is a distribution that has constant probability.

Applications

A common use of CIS studies is for methodological investigations of the performance of statistical estimators under various conditions. For instance, data are generated and models are estimated under several conditions (e.g., missing data, violation of certain assumptions). The performance of the estimators is compared in terms of parameter estimate bias, standard error bias, and coverage. A less common use of CISs is in deciding on sample size. The possibility of comparing various estimator distributions obtained for different sample sizes can prove useful in planning research by allowing the researcher to determine the sample size needed to achieve a desired precision level. CISs can also be used for power estimation, allowing comparison of the power attained using various estimators and/or sample sizes. In addition, unlike standard approaches to power estimation, which rely on numerous assumptions, including normal data distributions, computer-intensive power estimates make no distributional assumptions. CISs can also be used to study the effect of violation of assumptions on estimators and, consequently, on alpha-level, power, and confidence intervals. Researchers either can analyze "synthetic" data generated by assumed mathematical functions (e.g., random number generators), or they can utilize real-world data. At a minimum, CISs offer an additional perspective on determining sample size. Until the literature provides greater depth and breadth about the strengths and weakness of computer-intensive approaches, researchers should use these strategies as complements to power analysis and confidence intervals to determine sample size.

As discussed in chapter 1, because the sample is a part of a population, generalization from a sample to the population usually involves error. The traditional way of estimating sampling error is to start with an underlying population, which is assumed to have a certain distribution. Next, draw samples from this population, each of which, using a particular estimator (e.g., mean), will yield its own estimate. Then estimate how (i.e., according to which distribution) and how much (i.e., with how much variance) this estimator will fluctuate. This traditional approach to estimating sampling error tends to work for larger samples of characteristics with small variance. Often, however, researchers are unsure which underlying population distribution to assume. Computer-intensive techniques are rapidly entering mainstream data analysis; some researchers believe that these procedures will soon supplant common nonparametric procedures and could displace most parametric procedures as well (cf. Howell, 2007). Alternatively, CISs assume that sampling error can be estimated by drawing samples of the same size from the underlying distribution. That is, CISs provide access to a surrogate for the underlying distribution: the "empirical distribution" of a sample.

Strengths of Computer-Intensive Strategies

Some reasons cited by proponents for the use of computer-intensive methods as viable alternatives to classic inferential procedures are as follows:

1. Traditional inferential statistics requires distributional assumptions (e.g., shape). An inferential leap from a sample to its population can be problematic if there are reasons to suspect that assumptions are not tenable (Diaconis & Efron, 1983; Peterson, 1991).
2. CISs are more easily understood (Rudner & Shafer, 1992).

3. Classic inferential statistics requires random sampling to validate the inference from a sample to a population. Edington (1995), for example, argued that computer-intensive procedures are valid for any kind of data, including random and nonrandom data. More conservatively, Lunneborg (2000) observed that use of nonrandom samples with computer-intensive methods might not permit statistical inference but can provide descriptive information and a perspective on the stability of results.

4. CISs treat small samples as a virtual population to "generate" more observations (Helberg, 1996).

5. CISs can be used when there are too many participants (Helberg, 1996). Cohen (1969) has argued that the null hypothesis is inherently false because all things are different from each other to some extent and all things are also interrelated to some degree. According to Cohen, given a very large sample, virtually any null hypothesis can be rejected, no matter how practically trivial and meaningless it is.

6. According to Thompson and Snyder (1997), classical inferential procedures do not inform researchers about how likely the results are to be replicated. Repeated experiments in resampling, such as cross-validation and bootstrapping, can be used as internal replications.

Weaknesses of Computer-Intensive Strategies

1. When a sample does not conform to parametric assumptions, computer-intensive methods are recommended remedies (Diaconis & Efron, 1983). However, Good (1999) reminds researchers that CISs are still subject to the Behrens-Fisher problem, in which estimation is problematic when population variances are unknown. Specifically, both traditional tests and CI methods assume equal variances.

2. Some researchers are skeptical about the benefits of computer-intensive methods when used with nonrandom, nonrepresentative samples. If the sample that is used to generate the empirical sampling distribution does not reflect the characteristics of the population,

then the validity of the inference is compromised (Laudan, 1977). That is, nonrandom nonrepresentative samples are universal limitations (Rodgers, 1999). Moreover, Noreen (1989) pointed out that if the population conforms to the assumptions to derive the sampling distribution, then no other method, including CISs, can do any better than the conventional parametric tests.

3. Somewhat sarcastically, skeptics argue that CISs try "to get something for nothing. The same numbers are used over and over again until an answer is obtained that cannot be obtained by any other way" (Peterson, 1991).

4. Some observers question the accuracy of computer-intensive procedures. That is, in some situations, these procedures can be less accurate than conventional parametric methods (Stine, 1989). Computer-intensive methods, for example, fail for markedly nonlinear statistics such as the sample median (Efron, 1982). Some critics have argued that when the collected data are biased, computer-intensive methods can replicate and magnify error (cf. Ludbrook & Dudley, 1998; Rodgers, 1999).

5. Parametric assumptions have been shown to be relatively unimportant in a variety of contexts. That is, classical tests, such as t-tests, are robust against violations of the assumption of a normal distribution (cf. Pearson & Please, 1975).

In summary, CISs are not panaceas. Similar to other approaches to determining sample size, such as power analysis, CISs assume that the observations in the sample are independent. In addition, these strategies require a kind of parametric assumptions. That is, if it can be assumed that a sample is a reasonable representation of the population from which it was drawn, then these data can be used to reproduce a population under a null, and then multiple samples can be drawn from this population.

CISs are potentially useful because they can be applied to a wide range of statistical models, regardless of the model's complexity. These strategies also seem to be potentially viable approaches to help researchers determine sample size. For example, CISs can enable researchers to

(1) derive power and confidence intervals empirically; (2) access procedures that require a data set (e.g., confidence intervals for ANOVA), and (3) explore the effects of factors such as distributional assumptions and missing data.

CISs can enable social work researchers to learn more about their data. A recent example in social work is Guo and Hussey's (2004) Monte Carlo study using a multiple regression to explore the consequences of using nonprobability sampling procedures. By allowing social work researchers to begin asking and answering "what would happen if" questions, these techniques can enable them to begin to refine the process of determining sample size. The following example demonstrates how this process might work and encourage researchers to use more sophisticated resources, such as Stata and Matlab.

Example: A Computer-Intensive Strategy to Determine Sample Size

The strategy can be summarized as follows:

1. Use a random generator to construct a data set with variables of a given central tendency and dispersion.
2. Select multiple samples r of size n_1.
3. Run an analysis on each of r samples.
4. Calculate a summary measure based on these r samples.
5. Select r number of samples of a different size n_2.
6. Repeat steps 3 and 4.
7. Compare power and CIS samples n_1 and n_2.

Several decisions need to be made to carry out a Monte Carlo study. The first is the choice of the model to be studied. This choice is driven by the research question being asked. Once the model is chosen, population values for each parameter of the model must be selected. These values can be obtained from theory or from previous research. Estimates from previous studies are often the best estimates available for population values in the Monte Carlo study. Technical considerations in the Monte

Carlo study are the number of samples to be drawn and the seed. The number of samples to be drawn (replications) can be thought of as the sample size for the Monte Carlo study. The number of replications should be increased until stability of the results is achieved. The value of the seed determines the starting point for the random draws of the samples. More than one seed should be used, and the results for the different seeds should be checked for stability.

Accordingly, as a first step, a data set is constructed. These data can be constructed using a random number generator from a standard statistical package such as SPSS. For example, the following syntax generates 2,000 cases with three normally distributed variables.

```
set seed = 200409281.
input program.
loop #i = 1 to 2000.
compute x_normal = rv.normal(50,15).
compute y_normal = rv.normal(25,7).
compute z_normal = rv.normal(5,2).
end case.
end loop.
end file.
end input program.
formats x_normal (f8.4).
execute.
descriptives variables = x_normal y_normal z_normal /
   statistics = all.
```

One free program for generating data that conforms to user specifications is DataSim. With this software, users can generate individual and group-level data and specify the correlations among individuals and groups. DataSim is free and can be downloaded from the following web page: http://www.people.cornell.edu/pages/mcs5/Pages/DataSimPage .htm. Another resource for generating random numbers from a normal distribution with a selected mean and standard deviation is http://graphpad.com/quickcalcs/randomN1.cfm.

Assume that a researcher is planning a study of 20 participants in a parent effectiveness training program and 20 members of a comparison group. For each participant, data are available from a posttest measure of knowledge of child development. For simplicity, this example contains two variables, group and posttest, for 40 cases. The researcher would like to compare experimental and control group participants in terms of posttest means. A larger mean is expected for the experimental group as a result of the training. These data are summarized as follows: posttest mean experimental group = 29.5, posttest mean control group = 28.2, posttest standard deviation experimental group = 2.48, posttest standard deviation control group = 3.0.

1. Select 40 samples of size 40.
2. Perform an independent t-test on each the 40 samples.
3. Summarize the results of these 40 independent t-tests.
4. Select 40 samples of size 20.
5. Repeat steps 3 and 4.
6. Compare the summary results for the samples of $N = 40$ with the samples of $N = 20$. Specifically, define power as the percentage of samples with $p < .05$, and define confidence intervals as the average of the confidence intervals obtained for $N = 40$ samples and $N = 20$ samples.

Analyses were performed in two ways: using Simstat and an SPSS syntax file. Additional information about Simstat is available from http://www.provalisresearch.com/simstat/simstatv.html.

Simstat is traditional statistical package. It will resample data, perform statistical analyses on these samples, and extract and summarize results.

The SPSS syntax file is as follows:

```
DEFINE repsamp ().
!DO !doover = 1 !TO 40.
USE ALL.
```

```
do if $casenum=1.
compute #s_$_1=40.
compute #s_$_2=1000.
end if.
do if #s_$_2 > 0.
compute filter_$ = uniform(1) * #s_$_2 < #s_$_1.
compute #s_$_1 = #s_$_1–filter_$.
compute #s_$_2 = #s_$_2–1.
else.
compute filter_$ = 0.
end if.
VARIABLE LABEL filter_$ '10 from the first 1000 cases
    (SAMPLE).'
FORMAT filter_$ (f1.0).
FILTER BY filter_$.
T-TEST
GROUPS – group(1 0)
    /MISSING = ANALYSIS
    /VARIABLES = posttest
    /CRITERIA = CI (.95).
!DOEND.
!ENDDEFINE.
repsamp.
execute.
```

* Line 2 directs SPSS to draw 40 samples
*Line 5 directs SPSS to draw samples of N = 40
*Line 6 defines the number of cases in the sample as 1,000.

Results of these analyses are summarized as follows:

1. The 95% confidence interval was calculated by averaging the difference and standard error for two groups on posttest scores. For $N = 40$, the 95% confidence interval is $1.14 +/- 2(0.140) =$

1.21 – 1.78. For $N = 20$, the 95% confidence interval is 1.14 +/– 2(0.18) = 1.13 – 1.90. These confidence intervals suggest that a sample size of 20 might be sufficient.

2. Power was calculated by counting the number of instances in which a random sample achieved a significant t-value ($p < .05$). This total was expressed as a fraction of the total number of random samples that were drawn. In effect, power is defined as the percentage of times that the null hypothesis of no difference between the group means on the dependent variable was rejected. For $N = 40$, power equaled 0.82; for $N = 20$, power equaled 0.47.

Therefore, in contrast to the aforementioned confidence interval analysis, a sample size of 40 is necessary to approximately achieve the desired power of 0.80. To make a final decision about sample size, the researcher should weigh precision, power, and costs to both the respondent and the project. Although there are no easy answers, a consideration of at least these three factors could increase the likelihood of an ethically sound, efficient, and valid study.

Recommended Approach(es): Although CISs are conceptually simple, they require appropriate software. Computer-intensive methods can be implemented with specialized software, such as Resampling Stats,[1] or with extensions of general purpose packages, such as Matlab, Excel, Simstat, SAS, and SPSS. For example, free and adaptable syntax and macros for performing resampling in SPSS and SAS are available on the Internet.[2] Howell's (2007) text contains a very readable chapter on resampling. Howell also provides a free program that implements and demonstrates several resampling strategies. This program can be downloaded from http://www.uvm.edu/~dhowell/StatPages/Resampling/Resampling.html. Social workers interested in exploring resampling strategies might begin with David Howell's free resampling software.[3] Howell's software contains procedures for performing bootstrap procedures for means, medians, comparing two medians, correlations, and one-way ANOVA. For additional discussion of CISs, see Efron and Tibshirani (1993), Good (1999), and Sprent (1998).

In summary, this chapter (1) provided a brief description of the rationale and limitations of CISs, (2) presented an example of how CISs can be used to determine sample size, and (3) identified additional CISs related resources. In the next chapter, additional considerations, including ethics, costs, and balancing power and precision, are discussed. Finally, recommendations are presented.

5

Additional Considerations, Recommendations, and Conclusions

This chapter is organized into two sections. First, additional considerations that can affect sample size are discussed, including ethical concerns, costs, and synthesis of power and precision. Second, recommendations concerning future efforts to refine tactics and techniques for determining sample size are presented.

Additional Considerations

Ethical Criteria and Sample Size

Research places demands on participants in terms of privacy, time, and effort. Consequently, a study with a sample size that is too large or too small can raise ethical questions. More specifically, researchers should avoid conducting studies that are "underpowered." An underpowered study is one for which the projected scientific or clinical value is unacceptably low because it has less than an 80% chance of producing $p < .05$ under an assumed minimum important effect size. Conversely, researchers should avoid conducting studies with too large a sample size.

Studies with samples that are too large can needlessly place respondents at risk. It has been argued here that researchers should focus on determining the smallest necessary sample size.

Bacchetti, Wolf, Segal, and McCulloch (2005a, 2005b) discuss how sample size influences the balance that determines the *ethical acceptability* of a study—that is, the balance between the burdens that participants accept and the clinical or scientific value that a study can be expected to produce. The average projected burden per participant remains constant as the sample size increases, but the projected study value does not increase as rapidly as the sample size if it is assumed to be proportional to power or inversely proportional to confidence interval width. This implies that the value per participant declines as the sample size increases and that smaller studies therefore have more favorable ratios of projected value to participant burden. Bacchetti et al. (2005a, 2005b) provocatively conclude that that their argument "does not imply that large studies are never ethical or that small studies are better, only that a small study is ethically acceptable whenever a larger one is" (p. 113).

Analysis by Bacchetti et al. (2005a, 2005b) addresses only ethical acceptability, not optimality; large studies may be desirable for other than ethical reasons. The balance point between burden and value cannot be precisely calculated in most situations because both the projected participant burden and the study's projected value are difficult to quantify, particularly on comparable scales. Bacchetti et al. (2005a, 2005b) provided a service by encouraging researchers to think of value and burden on a per-participant basis and by arguing that the expected net burden per participant may often be independent of sample size (Prentice, 2005).

Institutional review boards are becoming more sophisticated regarding power and sample size issues, and, consequently, there could be fewer unnecessarily large studies in the future. For studies with higher risk, *sequential designs* should be considered. In a sequential design, data are analyzed periodically to determine whether sampling can be stopped and reliable conclusions drawn from the available data. In a sense, a sequential design allows the researcher to adjust sample size based on the accumulating results. Use of sequential designs is relatively common in medical research (Posch & Bauer, 2000; Whitehead, 1997), and these designs deserve increased consideration from social workers and other social science researchers. If a study seeks sensitive information or seeks to collect information during a crisis, it could be unethical to sample too many or too few people, and a sequential design can avoid over- and under-sampling.

Costs and Sample Size

Often, a study has a limited budget, which, at least in part, determines sample size. Consequently, sample design should aim to obtain maximum precision (minimum variance) for allowable costs (Kish, 1965). Some researchers have begun exploring design strategies that minimize costs while maintaining adequate power (see Schechtman & Gordon, 1993). Although it is not always possible to use cost criteria to determine sample size, costs can, at least, provide an additional perspective on sample size calculations.

Daniel and Terrel (1992) have suggested a formula for calculation of sample size with a fixed budget for a study. The sample size, n, is given by the formula $n = C - C_f/C_u$, where C represents the total budgeted cost of a sampling study, which can be broken into two parts: fixed cost, C_f, and the variable cost per sampling unit, C_u. Assuming an agency has a total budgeted cost that equals $5,000, variable cost (defined as the cost per questionnaire charged by a research consultant) equals $5 and fixed cost (agency personnel time) equals $1,500. Then $N = (5,000 - 1,500)/5 = 700$. Consequently, total budget costs for the study permit a sample size of 700.

Allison, Allison, Faith, Paultre, and Pi-sunyer (1997) describe a method of estimating the total research project costs that considers four levels of expenditures. For example, using the example described in chapter 4, assume a researcher is planning a study of participants of a parent effectiveness training program and members of a comparison group. To assess training effectiveness, each participant will be asked to complete a posttest measure of knowledge of child development. The first level, *basic overhead*, includes salaries for research staff and costs of equipment and supplies. The second level is the *cost of recruiting respondents*. Respondents can be recruited through mailings and newspaper advertisements. The third level is the *cost of treatment implementation* (i.e., parenting effectiveness training). The fourth level is the *cost of measuring the DV at the end of the study* (e.g., posttest measure of knowledge of child development).

An additional cost factor in surveys is response rate. In surveys, cost and response rate play an interrelated role in determining sample size. Although a 100% response rate always is desirable, it is not always a realistic expectation. Using follow-ups to increase response rate, such as telephone calls, postcards, or second and third repeat delivery of surveys, increases cost. An advantage of more expensive follow-up approaches, such as telephone calls, is that the response rate will be higher. Therefore, for a final sample size of 100 with a 75% return rate, the sample should include 133 respondents. For a detailed discussion of return rate and models of cost functions, see Kish (1965).

Balancing Power and Precision

Smithson (2001) argues that criteria for deciding on sample size should include the precision of the sample estimates, as well as the power to reject a null hypothesis. As discussed in chapter 2, if the researcher is determining sample size based on power, then the study design should ensure, to a high degree of certainty, that the study will be able to provide an adequate (i.e., powerful) testing of the null hypothesis. However, a study may be designed with another goal as well. In addition to (or instead of) testing the null hypothesis, study planning could focus on the precision with which the study will estimate the magnitude of the effect. The confidence interval (CI) represents the precision with which we are able to report the effect size; the larger the sample, the more precise the estimate. CIs provide different information from power analysis; high power does not always involve precise estimation. The key to understanding the difference between them is the realization that although significance level and sample size affect both power and interval width, effect size affects only power.

Precision analysis requires a criterion for acceptable CI width. However, these criteria have received little attention in the social sciences literature, and the establishment of acceptable benchmarks is necessary. Smithson (2001) suggests, as a beginning point, that researchers could rely on Cohen's (1988) benchmarks. For example, for R^2, .01 = small, .09 = medium, and .25 = large. Consequently, when $R^2 = .05$, the lower limit of the 95% CI should exceed .09, which is akin to being able to distinguish a large from a medium effect. In addition, when $R^2 = .10$, the upper limit of the 95% CI should fall below .25, and the lower limit should exceed .01.

Using both power and precision to determine sample size is, according to Smithson (2001), not a commonly utilized strategy. Researchers might consider exploring power before conducting a study and then supplementing that exploration with an investigation of CI width.

Recommendations

Power analysis, CI estimation, and computer-intensive methods suggest that "adequate" sample size (e.g., >.80) can be an expensive commodity. Authors such as Lenth (2001) and Parker and Berman (2003) suggest that a "sufficient" sample is only one component of a study's quality. Other important considerations include the validity of a study's model, measurement, and design. The aforementioned authors explain that, traditionally, sample size calculations have been viewed as calculations to determine the correct number of respondents needed for a study. These calculations focus on statements such as "for a difference X, sample size Y is needed." Lenth (2001) and Parker and Berman (2003), however, argue that for many studies, a focus on statements such as "for a sample size Y, information Z is obtained" is more appropriate.

With the aforementioned perspective in mind, social work researchers should consider the following recommendations:

General Strategies

1. Authors should always provide detailed descriptions of the samples. Detailed description is necessary to understand the population being studied and to judge whether the extent of generalizing results seems appropriate. Also, when possible, a comparison of study participants and information about the population should be provided to enable readers to evaluate a sample's representativeness in terms of the larger population from which it was drawn. This comparative information is especially important when nonrandom samples are used. With nonrandom samples external validity is best evaluated by judging the logical probability that other populations share the relevant characteristics of the individuals who did not participate in a given study. Moreover, detailed information about a study's sample is essential as techniques for combining the results of multiple studies, such as meta-analysis, become more widely accepted (Glass, McGaw, & Smith, 1981; Hedges & Olkin, 1985; Hunter, Schmidt, & Jackson, 1982).
2. A pilot study should be conducted when estimates needed for power analysis, CIs, and resampling are not available.
3. Multiple approaches to calculating appropriate effect-size values and corresponding sample sizes should be used. Within the context of a specific study, investigators should seek a perspective on the benefits and limitations of a range of sample sizes to their ability to answer their research questions. One strategy might be to begin with a sample size and, through resampling, explore the consequences of incremental changes in sample size on power and CIs.
4. Researchers should plan in advance and in detail for data analysis (Assman, Pocock, Enos, & Kasten, 2000). The more statistical tests that are performed, the more likely it is that a statistically significant result will be found. This phenomenon results from performing multiple, unplanned statistical tests and is variously termed *alpha decay, probability pyramiding, or capitalizing on chance* (see Pocock, Geller, & Tsiatis, 1987). It is not suggested here that exploratory analysis cannot be a valuable knowledge building tool. It

is, however, recommended that descriptive, predictive, and explanatory investigations should be preplanned and should include detailed descriptions of data analysis procedures.

5. For ethical and efficiency concerns, social work researchers should consider evaluating conditional power at various points in the data collection process and stopping data collection early if, for example, there is either a strong treatment effect or strong evidence of no treatment effect. That is, *conditional power* is the probability that the final study result will be statistically significant, given data observed up to a point in a study. For example, a conditional power computation performed at a prespecified point in the study, such as at the midpoint, can be used as the basis for early termination when there is little evidence of a beneficial effect or if it appears that results have begun to stabilize (cf. Betensky, 1997; Lachin, 2005; Shih, 2001).

Use Random Sample or Generalize Outside a Sample Only With Caution

Social work researchers should make every effort to incorporate a random process as a component of a sampling strategy. Nonrandom sampling strategies present significant limitations to the use of power analysis and CI estimation, because these strategies assume that data are obtained through a random process. Generalizing from a nonrandom sample to a population could yield biased conclusions. With large samples, this limitation of nonrandom samples can seem counterintuitive. Nonetheless, even large-scale studies based on nonrandom sampling schemes can yield biased conclusions. See, for example, Winship and Mare (1992) for a conceptualization of sample selection bias and Guo and Hussey (2004) for a recent Monte Carlo study and discussion of these issues. The essential problem with nonrandom samples is that respondents selected for the sample could differ systematically from their population of interest. It is not suggested here that useful insights cannot be gained from nonrandomly selected data. It is important, however, that inferences from nonrandom samples be made with great care.

With a body of evidence that relies heavily on nonrandom samples, "streams of research" are particularly important. Kruglanski (1975) argued that multiple studies aimed at investigating interrelated aspects of a phenomenon using different samples might generate more confidence in any single study's findings. Considering the ethical and logistical barriers to obtaining random samples, combing the findings from a reasonably large set of nonprobability samples might be an acceptable, practical compromise.

Differential Use of Smaller Versus Larger Samples

Bannister (1981), Hoyle (1999), and Isaac and Michael (1995) provide guidance about the benefits of smaller versus larger samples. According to Isaac and Michael (1995), large samples are essential in the following instances:

1. A large number of uncontrolled variables are interacting unpredictably, and it is desirable to minimize their separate effects; that is, to mix the effects randomly and cancel out imbalances.
2. The total sample is to be subdivided into several subsamples to be compared with one another.
3. The parent population consists of a wide range of variables and characteristics, and there is a risk of missing or misrepresenting these differences.

According to Isaac and Michael (1995), small sample sizes are justifiable in the following instances:

1. In exploratory research and pilot studies.
2. When the research seeks greater depth than breadth; for example, when unstructured in person interviews are used.
3. When methodological control is high.

In conclusion, this book presents approaches for determining sample size in social work research. Approaches described include power analysis, confidence intervals, and computer-intensive strategies. Other considerations are ethics, costs, and balancing power and precision. The focus here has been on quantitative research in which a primary goal is to use statistical inference to generalize results obtained from a sample to a population. In these investigations, the preference is for a sampling design that will yield estimated effect sizes with the least amount of associated error.

Sample size planning is always important and almost always difficult. Accordingly, social work researchers should consider using multiple approaches to estimating sample size. Pressure to increase sample size can be mitigated by (1) a view that, in terms of fewer dependent and independent variables, simpler study designs are better; (2) an emphasis on replication; and (3) carefully planned analyses. If, ultimately, assumptions for a particular statistical procedure are untenable, researchers should frame study conclusions accordingly.

6

Worked Examples

The following examples demonstrate a priori sample size determination strategies presented in previous chapters. Specifically, for each procedure, minimum sample size will be estimated with power analysis and confidence intervals (CIs). Free software, including GPower; commercial software; and web-based calculators will be used to demonstrate the range of resources available for estimating minimum sample size. Sample sizes based on power analysis and CIs should be considered within the context of ethical and cost-related issues. See Table 1.1 in chapter 1 for a summary of discussion and examples by procedure, and Table 1.2 for a summary of effect-size measures discussed in previous chapters.

Note that, because of space limitations, computer-intensive strategies are not demonstrated in this chapter. However, a detailed example is provided in chapter 4. A brief summary of the example in chapter 4 is as follows:

1. Select r samples of size N_1.
2. Perform an independent t-test on each the 40 samples.
3. Summarize the results of these 40 independent t-tests.
4. Select r samples of size N_2.

5. Repeat steps 3 and 4.

6. Compare the summary results for the samples of N_1 with the samples of N_2. Specifically, define power as the percentage of samples with $p < .05$, and define CIs as the average of the CIs obtained for N_1 samples and N_2 samples.

Analyses can be performed in at least two ways, using either Simstat or an SPSS syntax file (see chapter 4 for a copy of this syntax file). Additional information about Simstat is available from http://www .provalisresearch.com/simstat/simstatv.html. Simstat is a traditional statistical package. It will resample data, perform statistical analyses on these samples, and extract and summarize results.

Example 1: Difference Between Two Means—Independent Samples

Power Analysis

A researcher is planning a study to compare the effectiveness of two treatments for spouse abusers. Treatment A consists of a group treatment for abusers. Treatment B consists of group treatment for abusers and their partners. Participants will be randomly assigned to groups, and groups will have an equal number of participants. After completing the treatment, spouse abusers will be administered an "empathy" scale. Higher scores indicate higher levels of empathy. The researcher anticipates a medium effect size of $d = 0.5$. Table 6.1 and Figures 6.1 and 6.2 summarize a power analysis for this study in GPower. A complete GPower user's manual is available at http://www.psycho.uni-duesseldorf .de/aap/projects/gpower/how_to_use_gpower.html.

Confidence Intervals

Based on previous research and the sample size used in the previous example, assume mean$_1$ = 10, mean$_2$ = 12, the standard deviation (*SD*)

Table 6.1

Select	*t*-test (means)	
	Type of power analysis	A priori
	Type of test	*t*-test (means), two-tailed
		Accuracy mode calculation
Input	Effect size *d*	0.5
		Note that to calculate the effect size from mean A, mean B, and the pooled standard deviation, click "Calc d," insert the means and the standard deviation, and click "Calc & Copy."
	Alpha	.05
	Power (1 − beta)	.8
Click Calculate		
Result	Total sample size	102
	Actual power	.8059
	Critical *t*	1.6602
	Delta	Noncentrality parameter = 2.5249

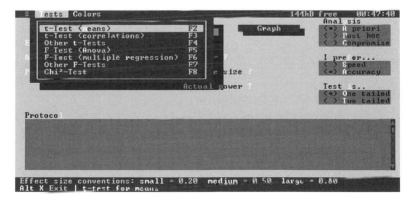

Figure 6.1. Selecting a Test in GPower

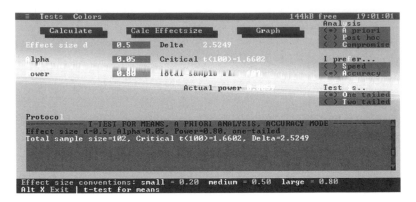

Figure 6.2. GPower Input and Results

for both means = 3.5, and N = 102, or 51 in each group. The web-based
calculator at http://graphpad.com/quickcalcs/ErrorProp1.cfm?Format=
SD yields the following: 95% CI: 0.62 to 3.38 (see Figures 6.3 and 6.4).

Example 2: Difference Between Two Means—Correlated Samples

Power Analysis

A researcher is planning a study to evaluate the effectiveness of a group
treatment for spouse abusers. Before and after completing the treatment, spouse abusers will be administered an "empathy" scale. Higher
scores indicate higher levels of empathy. The researcher anticipates a medium effect size of $d = 0.5$ (e.g., increase in treatment scale scores as a
result of the treatment). Table 6.2 and Figures 6.5 and 6.6 summarize a
power analysis for this study in nQuery Advisor.

Confidence Intervals

Based on previous research and the sample size used in the previous
example, assume mean = 20, the *SD* for both means = 7, and N = 27.

GraphPad Software
ANALYZE, GRAPH AND ORGANIZE YOUR DATA

Try our
free demos

QuickCalcs Online Calculators for Scientists

1. Select category   2. Choose calculator   **3. Enter data**   4. View results

Compute CI of a sum, difference, quotient or product

This calculator computes confidence intervals of a sum, difference, quotient or product of two means, assuming both groups follow a Gaussian distribution.

1. Choose data entry format

⦿ Enter mean, N and SD.
○ Enter mean, N and SEM.
Caution: Changing format will erase your data.

2. Enter data

Variable name	Mean	SD	N
Variable A	12	3.5	51
Variable B	10	3.5	51

3. Which operation?

Calculate the confidence interval of:
○ A + B
⦿ A - B
○ A / B
○ A * B

4. View the results

Calculate now

Clear the form

Figure 6.3. Quick Calcs Input

GraphPad Software
ANALYZE, GRAPH AND ORGANIZE YOUR DATA

Try our
free demos

QuickCalcs Online Calculators for Scientists

1. Select category   2. Choose calculator   3. Enter data   **4. View results**

CI of a sum, difference, quotient or product

Mean of Variable A **minus** Mean of Variable B = 2.00

90% CI: 0.85 to 3.15

95% CI: 0.62 to 3.38

99% CI: 0.18 to 3.82

These results assume that both variables follow a Gaussian distribution and that the measurements of Variable A are not paired or matched to measurements of Variable B.

	Variable A	Variable B
Mean	12.00	10.00
SD	3.50	0.50
SEM	0.49	0.49
N	51	51

Figure 6.4. Quick Calcs Results

Table 6.2

Select	Goal	Means
	Number of groups	One
	Analysis method	Test
		Paired t-test for differences in means
Input	Alpha	.05
	One- or two-sided test	One
	Effect size d	0.5
	Power (%)	80
	Click on blank cell adjacent to n to calculate	
	n	27

Table 6.3 summarizes the calculation of a 95% CI for this study in nQuery Advisor.

Therefore, the 95% CI is 7.0 minus 2.64 to 7.0 plus 2.64, or 4.36 to 9.64 (see Figures 6.7 and 6.8).

Example 3: Differences Between Independent Proportions

Power Analysis

A researcher is planning to study the relationship between going to college and working. She posits that 50% of full-time college students work at least 20 hours per week compared with 80% percent of part-time students. Table 6.4 summarizes a power analysis for this study using a web-based calculator located at http://statpages.org/proppowr.html.

Note that this page incorporates a continuity correction to the usual sample size formula based on the normal approximation to the binomial distribution. This correction increases the sample size (for each group) by an amount approximately equal to $2/\text{abs}(p_1 - p_2)$, where p_1 and p_2 are the population proportions for the two groups (see Figure 6.9).

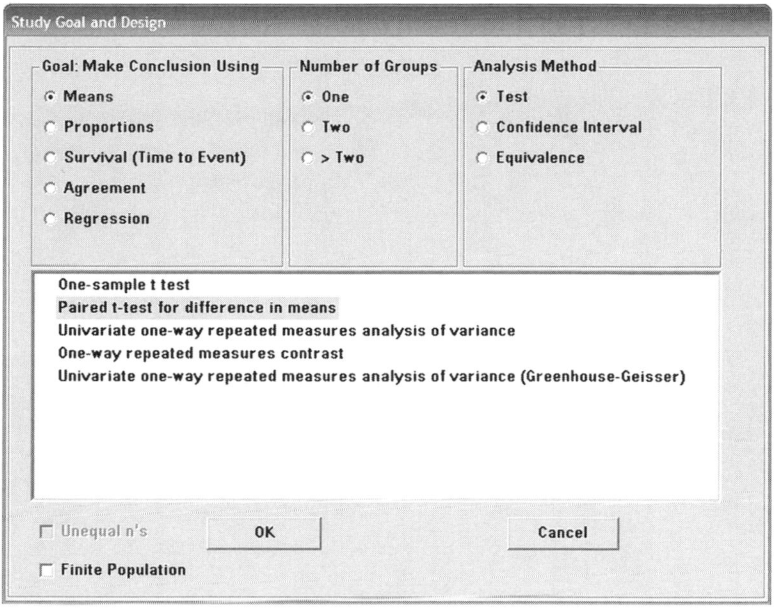

Figure 6.5. Selecting a Test in nQuery Advisor

	1	2	3
Test significance level, α	0.050		
1 or 2 sided test?	1		
First condition mean, μ_1			
Second condition mean, μ_2			
Mean difference, $\mu_d = \mu_1 - \mu_2$			
Standard deviation of differences, σ_d			
Effect size, $\delta = |\mu_d| / \sigma_d$	0.500		
Power (%)	80		
n	27		

Figure 6.6. nQuery Advisor Results

Table 6.3

Select	Goal	Means
	Number of groups	One
	Analysis method	Confidence interval
		Confidence interval for differences in paired means
Input	Alpha	.05
	CI	.95
	One- or two-sided interval	Two
	SD of difference scores	7.0
	n	27
	Click on blank cell adjacent to n to calculate	
Result	Distance to mean	2.64

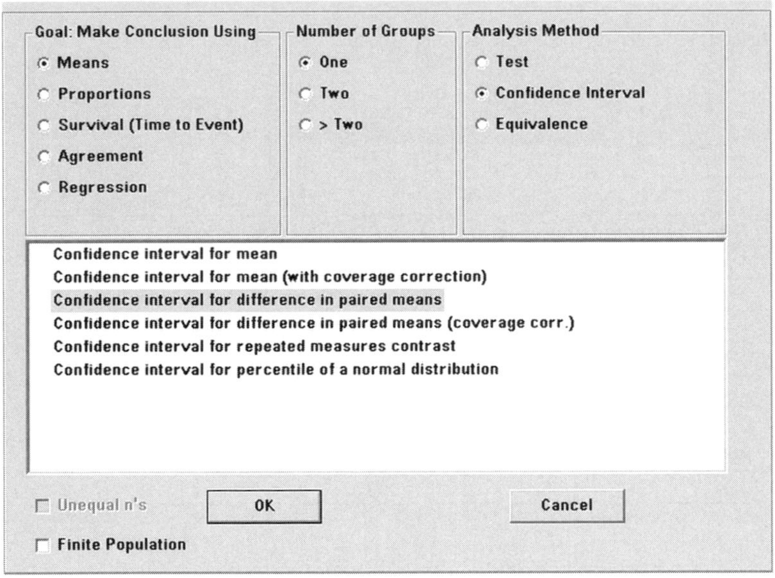

Figure 6.7. Selecting a Test in nQuery Advisor

	1	2	3
Confidence level, 1-α	0.950		
1 or 2 sided interval?	2		
Standard deviation of differences, σ_d	7.000		
Distance from mean to limit, ω	2.640		
n	27		

Figure 6.8. nQuery Advisor Results

Confidence Intervals

The following web page calculates the confidence interval for the difference between two independent proportions: http://faculty.vassar.edu/
lowry/prop2_ind.html. Assuming the aforementioned study, this calculator yields the following result: 95% CI is .1691 to .4170 (see Figure
6.10).

Example 4: Odds Ratio

Power Analysis

A researcher is planning to study the relationship between going to
college and working. She posits that 50% of full-time college students
work at least 20 hours per week compared with 80% of part-time

Table 6.4

Input	Alpha	.05
	Power (% chance of detecting)	80
	First group population proportion	0.5
	Second group population proportion	0.8
	Relative sample sizes required (Group 2/Group 1)	1.0
Result	Sample size required (For equal samples, use 1.0)	Group 1: 45 Group 2: 45

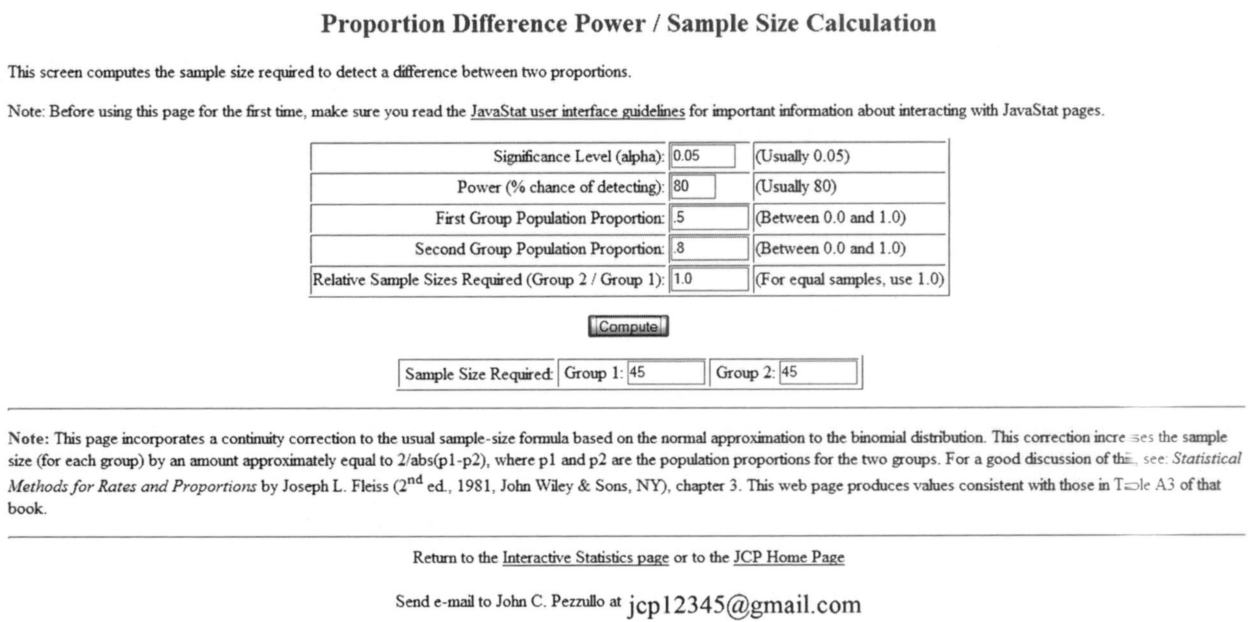

Proportion Difference Power / Sample Size Calculation

This screen computes the sample size required to detect a difference between two proportions.

Note: Before using this page for the first time, make sure you read the JavaStat user interface guidelines for important information about interacting with JavaStat pages.

Significance Level (alpha):	0.05	(Usually 0.05)
Power (% chance of detecting):	80	(Usually 80)
First Group Population Proportion:	.5	(Between 0.0 and 1.0)
Second Group Population Proportion:	.8	(Between 0.0 and 1.0)
Relative Sample Sizes Required (Group 2 / Group 1):	1.0	(For equal samples, use 1.0)

Compute

Sample Size Required:	Group 1:	45	Group 2:	45

Return to the Interactive Statistics page or to the JCP Home Page

Send e-mail to John C. Pezzullo at jcp12345@gmail.com

Note: This page incorporates a continuity correction to the usual sample-size formula based on the normal approximation to the binomial distribution. This correction increases the sample size (for each group) by an amount approximately equal to 2/abs(p1-p2), where p1 and p2 are the population proportions for the two groups. For a good discussion of this, see: *Statistical Methods for Rates and Proportions* by Joseph L. Fleiss (2nd ed., 1981, John Wiley & Sons, NY), chapter 3. This web page produces values consistent with those in Table A.3 of that book.

Figure 6.9. Interactive Statistics Page Input and Results

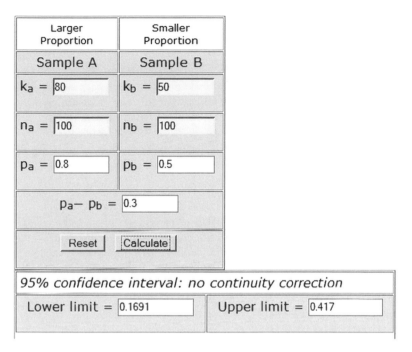

Larger Proportion	Smaller Proportion
Sample A	Sample B
k_a = 80	k_b = 50
n_a = 100	n_b = 100
p_a = 0.8	p_b = 0.5

$p_a - p_b$ = 0.3	
Reset	Calculate

95% confidence interval: no continuity correction

Lower limit = 0.1691	Upper limit = 0.417

Figure 6.10. VasarStats Input and Results

students. That is, the odds ratio equals 4.00. Table 6.5 summarizes a power analysis for this study in nQuery Advisor.

Note that this example also suggests that odds ratios can sometimes seem to overstate relative positions: in this sample, part-time college students have four times the odds of full-time college students of working at least 20 hours per week (see Figures 6.11 and 6.12).

Confidence Intervals

A researcher is planning to study the relationship between going to college and working. She posits that 50% of full-time college students work at least 20 hours per week compared with 80% of part-time students. That is, the odds ratio equals 4.00. Using the calculator located

Table 6.5

Select	Goal	Proportions
	Number of groups	Two
	Analysis method	Test
		Chi-square to compare two proportions
		Compute power or sample size
Input	Alpha	.05
	One- or two-sided test	Two
	Group 1 proportion	0.5
	Group 2 proportion	0.8
	Odds ratio	4.00
	Power (%)	80
	Click on blank cell adjacent to *n* to calculate	
Result	*N* per group	39

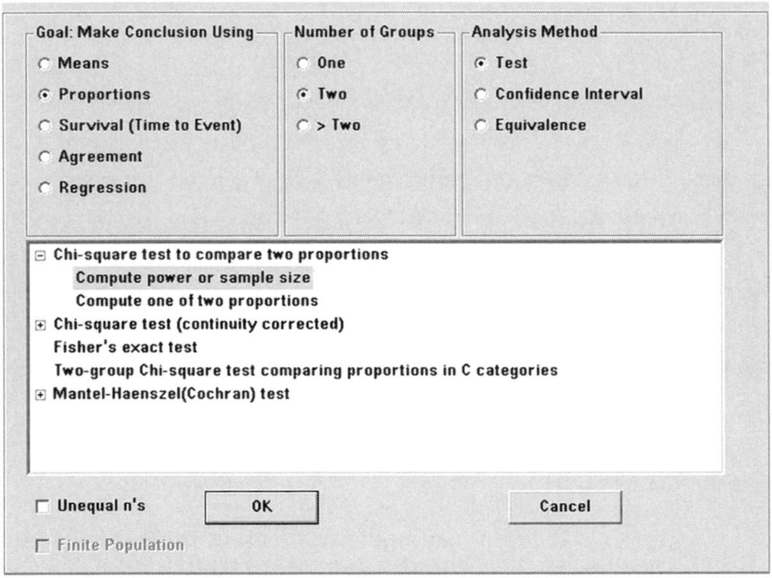

Figure 6.11. Selecting a Test in nQuery Advisor

	1	2	3
Test significance level, α	0.050		
1 or 2 sided test?	2		
Group 1 proportion, π_1	0.500		
Group 2 proportion, π_2	0.800		
Odds ratio, $\psi = \pi_2 (1 - \pi_1) / [\pi_1 (1 - \pi_2)]$	4.000		
Power (%)	80		
n per group	39		

Figure 6.12. nQuery Results

at http://www.hutchon.net/ConfidORselect.htm, the 95% CI is 2.1357 to 7.4917 (see Figure 6.13).

Example 5: Chi-Square and Contingency Tables (Test of Independence)

Power Analysis

A researcher is planning to study the relationship between going to college and working. She posits a medium effect size of $w = .30$. Table 6.6 and Figures 6.14 and 6.15 summarize a power analysis for this study in GPower.

Confidence Intervals

Assuming the aforementioned study with degrees of freedom $(df) = 1$ and chi-square $= 3.8413$, the following web-based calculator identifies whether it falls into a selected confidence range: http://www.hostsrv .com/webmaa/app1/MSP/webm1010/chi2. The chi-square statistic, 3.8415, is inside the 95% confidence interval. The 95% confidence interval for chi-square with 1 df is .0010 to 5.0238 (see Figure 6.16).

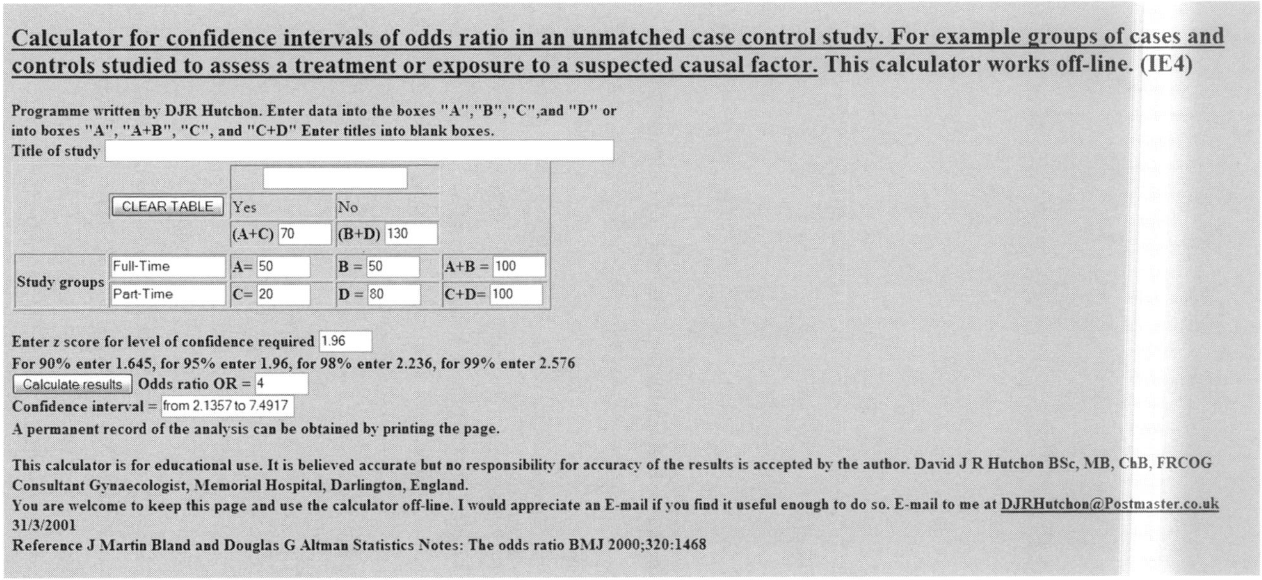

Calculator for confidence intervals of odds ratio in an unmatched case control study. For example groups of cases and controls studied to assess a treatment or exposure to a suspected causal factor. This calculator works off-line. (IE4)

Programme written by DJR Hutchon. Enter data into the boxes "A", "B", "C", and "D" or into boxes "A+B", "C", and "C+D" Enter titles into blank boxes.

Title of study: _____

CLEAR TABLE

	Yes	No	
	(A+C) 70	(B+D) 130	
Study groups	Full-Time	A= 50	B = 50	A+B = 100
	Part-Time	C= 20	D= 80	C+D= 100

Enter z score for level of confidence required 1.96
For 90% enter 1.645, for 95% enter 1.96, for 98% enter 2.236, for 99% enter 2.576

Calculate results   Odds ratio OR = 4

Confidence interval = from 2.1357 to 7.4917

A permanent record of the analysis can be obtained by printing the page.

This calculator is for educational use. It is believed accurate but no responsibility for accuracy of the results is accepted by the author. David J R Hutchon BSc, MB, ChB, FRCOG Consultant Gynaecologist, Memorial Hospital, Darlington, England.
You are welcome to keep this page and use the calculator off-line. I would appreciate an E-mail if you find it useful enough to do so. E-mail to me at DJRHutchon@Postmaster.co.uk
31/3/2001
Reference J Martin Bland and Douglas G Altman Statistics Notes: The odds ratio BMJ 2000;320:1468

Figure 6.13. Input and Results from http://www.hutchon.net

Table 6.6

Select	Type of test	Chi-square
	Type of power analysis	A priori
		Accuracy mode calculation
Input	Effect size w	0.3
	Alpha	0.05
	Power	0.80
	df	$(\text{rows} - 1) \times (\text{columns} - 1) = 1 \times 1 = 1$
Result	Lambda	7.9200
	Critical chi-square	$(1) = 3.8415$
	Total sample size	88
	Actual power	0.8035

Example 6: ANOVA, Fixed Effects, Single Factor

Power Analysis

A researcher is planning a study to compare the level of self-esteem among Anglo, African American, and Mexican American juvenile offenders (i.e., three groups) in a substance abuse treatment program. After completing the treatment, program participants will be administered

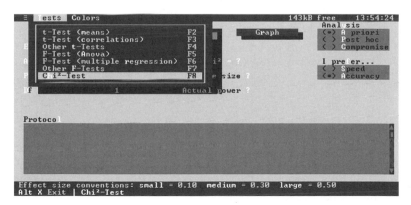

Figure 6.14. Selecting a Test in GPower

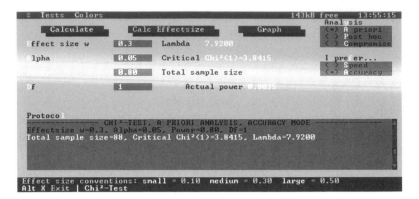

Figure 6.15. GPower Input and Results

a "self-esteem" scale. Higher scores indicate higher levels of self-esteem. The researcher anticipates a medium effect size of $f = 0.25$. Table 6.7 and Figures 6.17 and 6.18 summarize a power analysis for this study in GPower.

Confidence Intervals

Recall from chapter 3, page 46, that contrast coding creates a new variable by assigning numeric weights to the levels of an ANOVA factor under the constraint that the sum of the weights equals zero. Assuming the aforementioned study, a researcher plans to calculate the 95% CI of a contrast to compare the posttreatment level of self-esteem among Anglo and African American juvenile offenders with the level of self-esteem among Mexican American juvenile offenders (i.e., three groups). One way of expressing this is by: $\mu_1 + \mu_2 - 2(\mu_3)$, with coefficients $+1, +1, -2$. Note that these coefficients sum to zero. Table 6.8 and Figures 6.19 and 6.20 summarize the calculation of a 95% CI for this study in nQuery Advisor:

Even with the aid of statistical software, the calculation of a CI on a contrast is complex. Another strategy is to focus on a minimum power specification. Determining the CI on a contrast for an ANOVA design is usually difficult because of the need to specify all of the treatment means

Chi Square Tests

Given a chi square statistic this script identifies whether it falls into a selected confidence range.

- Confidence level:
  - ◇ ○ 99% confidence
  - ◇ ○ 98 % confidence
  - ◇ ● 95 % confidence
  - ◇ ○ 90 % confidence
  - ◇ ○ 80 % confidence
- Degrees of freedom: [1]
- Chi square statistic: [3.8413]
- One or two sided?:
  - ◇ ● one tail - high end
  - ◇ ○ one tail - low end
  - ◇ ○ two sided
- [Evaluate]

Script generated by MSPWizard.nb

Ken Levasseur
Mathematical Sciences
UMass Lowell
Kenneth_Levasseur@uml.edu
Ken's *WebMathematica Scripts*

The Chi-squared statistic, 3.8413 is inside the 95 % confidence interval. The 95 % confidence interval for Chi-squared with 1 degrees of freedom is (0.000982069, 5.02389)

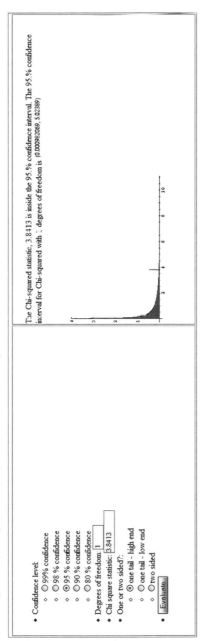

Figure 6.16. Webmathematica Input and Results

Table 6.7

Select	F-test (ANOVA)	
	Type of power analysis	A priori
	Type of test	F-test (ANOVA)
		Accuracy mode calculation
	Hypothesis	Global
Input	Effect size f	.25
	Alpha	0.05
	Beta	0.80
	Groups	3
Click Calculate		
Result	Lambda	9.9375
	Critical F	$(2,156) = 3.0540$
	Total sample size	159
	Actual power	0.8049

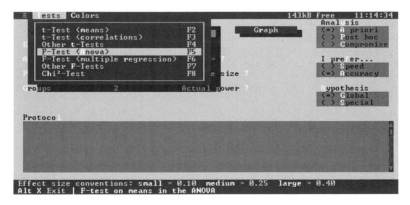

Figure 6.17. Selecting a Test in GPower

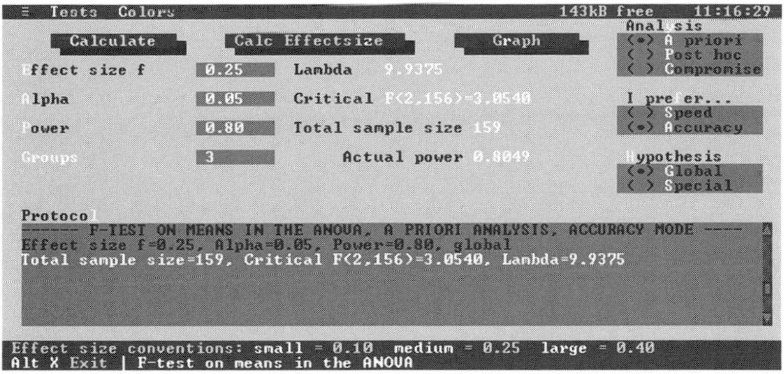

Figure 6.18. GPower Input and Results

Table 6.8

Select	Goal	Means
	Number of groups	>2
	Analysis method	Confidence interval
		Confidence interval width for one-way contrast
Input	CI	.95
	One- or two-sided interval	Two
	Number of groups	3
	Contrast	Using previous research or theory, the means for each group on the self-esteem scale must be specified
	Click on "compute effect size"	Enter group means 50, 60, 60; coefficients 1, 1, −2
	Click on "compute"	
	Click on "transfer"	
	Common standard deviation (assume they are equal)	5
	n per group	From preceding example = 53
	Click on blank cell adjacent to "distance from mean to limit"	
Result	Distance from mean to limit	3.297; therefore, the 95% CI is 6.708 to 13.297 (10.0 − 3.297 to 10.0 + 3.297)

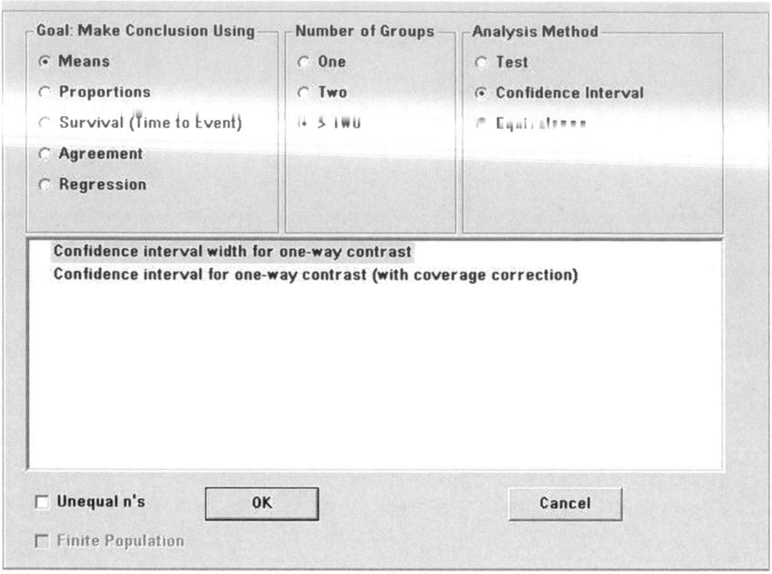

Figure 6.19. Selecting a Test in nQuery Advisor

	1	2	3
Confidence level, 1-α	0.950		
1 or 2 sided interval?	2		
Number of groups, G	3		
Contrast, $C = \Sigma c_i \mu_i$	-10.000		
Scale, $D = SQRT(\Sigma c_i^2)$	2.449		
Common standard deviation, σ	5.000		
Distance from mean to limit, ω	3.297		
n per group	53		

Figure 6.20. nQuery Advisor Results

and standard deviations. An alternative is to focus on the difference between the largest mean and the smallest mean. Although less precise in terms of determining sample size, this minimum power specification might be more feasible if there is little empirical experience with a phenomenon. Moreover, this minimum power specification corresponds to the alternative hypothesis that all means other than the two extreme ones are equal to the grand mean. In this way, the problem is reduced to calculating a CI for the difference between two means (see example 1 above).

Example 7a: ANCOVA

Power Analysis

A researcher is planning a study to compare changes in the level of self-esteem among Anglo, African American, and Mexican American juvenile offenders in a substance abuse treatment program (i.e., three groups), controlling for age (i.e., one covariate). After completing the treatment, program participants will be administered a self-esteem scale. Higher scores indicate higher levels of self-esteem. The researcher anticipates a medium effect size of $f = 0.25$.

In an analysis of covariance (ANCOVA), we replace a dependent variable Y with a corrected dependent variable Y', which we arrive at by partialing out the linear relation between Y and a set X of covariates. The ANCOVA is essentially an analysis of variance (ANOVA) of the Y' measures. However, we need to adjust the denominator df. If k is the number of groups in your design, enter groups $= k + q$ (q is the number of covariates in your design). In this way, the denominator df are reduced appropriately because GPower assumes that denominator $df = N - $ groups. Table 6.9 and Figures 6.21 and 6.22 summarize a power analysis for this study in GPower.

Table 6.9

Select	Type of test	F-test (ANOVA), special
	Type of power analysis	A priori
		Accuracy mode calculation
	Hypothesis	Special
Input	Effect size f	0.25
	Alpha	0.05
	Power	0.80
	[1]Groups	$3 + 1 = 4$
	[2]Numerator df	$3 - 1 = 2$
Result	Lambda	9.8750
	Critical F	$(2,154) = 3.0548$
	Total sample size	158
	Actual power $(1 - beta)$	0.8021

[1]Groups $= k$ (number of groups in the design) $+ q$ (the number of covariates in the design)

[2]Numerator $df =$ number of groups (*not* groups + covariates) minus $1 = k - 1$

Figure 6.21. Selecting a Test in GPower

```
≡ Tests  Colors                              143kB free    10:40:23
                                                    Analysis
     Calculate          Calc Effectsize          Graph       <•> A priori
                                                             < > Post hoc
  ffect size f     0.25     Lambda    9.8750               < > Compromise

  lpha             0.05     Critical F(2.154)=3.0548        I pre er...
                                                             < > Speed
  ower             0.80     Total sample size  158          <•> Accuracy

  roups            4        Actual power  0.8021            Hypothesis
                                                             < > Global
  Numerat r df     2                                        <•> Special

  Protocol
       F-TEST ON MEANS IN THE ANOVA. A PRIORI ANALYSIS. ACCURACY MODE
  Effect size f=0.25, Alpha=0.05, Power=0.80, special
  Total sample size=158, Critical F(2.154)=3.0548, Lambda=9.8750


  Effect size conventions: small = 0.10  medium = 0.25  large = 0.40
  Alt X Exit  | F-test on means in the ANOVA
```

Figure 6.22. GPower Input and Results

Example 7b: ANCOVA

Power Analysis

If the correlation between Y and the covariates is substantial, then the power of your statistical test is increased. This is so because the within-population SD sigma $_{Y'}$ in the denominator of the F ratio is smaller than sigma $_Y$. Specifically, where r is the (multiple) population correlation between Y' and Y, we find that SD of $_{Y'}$ equals SD_Y times the square root of $1 - r^2$. The numerator does not decrease correspondingly; it may even increase. This example is an illustration of how to utilize $SD_{Y'} = SD_Y$ times the square root of $1 - r^2$ to estimate sample size. The following strategy is possible when a researcher is able to estimate (1) the group means on the dependent variable and (2) the correlation between a covariate and the dependent variable. This example follows a strategy suggested by Wuensch (2006).

A researcher wants to a conduct a one-way ANCOVA (one factor or treatment condition) with three levels (groups) and one single covariate. She needs to estimate sample size for power of .80, alpha of .05, and a medium effect size (f=.25).

Assuming no covariates, Cohen's f (effect size) is computed as

$$\sqrt{\frac{\sum (\mu_j - \mu)^2 / k}{\sigma_e^2}}.$$

Cohen suggests that a medium-sized difference between two groups is one that equals one half the size of the within-group (error) variance, such as when $\mu_1 = 16$, $\mu_2 = 24$, $\mu = 20$, and $\sigma = 16$. This corresponds to a value of f equal to

$$\sqrt{\frac{(4^2 + 4^2)/2}{16^2}} = 0.25,$$

which is exactly the value of f that Cohen has suggested corresponds to a medium-sized effect in ANOVA.

Sample size equals

$$\phi = f\sqrt{n},$$

where n is the number of scores in each group. From Howell (2007, Appendix ncF, p. 675), $dft = 1$, $a = .05$, a ϕ of approximately 2 is needed, and therefore,

$$n = \left(\frac{\phi}{f}\right)^2 = \left(\frac{2}{.25}\right)^2 = 64.$$

Including a covariate will increase power for a fixed sample size because the error variance (the variance of the dependent variable scores after being adjusted for the covariate) will be reduced; the larger the correlation between the covariate and the dependent variable (or, with multiple covariates, the multiple R between covariates and the dependent variable), the greater the reduction of error variance. The error variance of the adjusted scores equals

$$\sigma_{Yadj} = \sigma_Y \sqrt{1 - r^2}.$$

Assuming a correlation between the covariate and the dependent variable of .5, $y_{adj} = 16\sqrt{1 - .25} = 13.86$.

Adjusting the value of f to reflect the reduction in error variance because of the covariate, the adjusted f equals

$$\sqrt{\frac{(4^2 + 4^2)/2}{13.86^2}} = .29,$$

and the required sample size equals

$$n = \left(\frac{2}{.29}\right)^2 = 48$$

participants in each group; that is, 48 participants at each level of each independent variable, or $3 \times 48 = 144$. Notice that specifying a correlation of .50 between the covariate and the dependent variable reduces the sample size from 158 (see example 7a) to 144.

Confidence Intervals

One strategy is to compute the CI for a contrast as described previously for an ANOVA model (see example 6) and consider this CI as a conservative estimate of the true CI of the ANCOVA. Another strategy is to focus on a minimum power specification; that is, focus on the difference between the largest mean and the smallest mean. Although less precise in terms of determining sample size, this minimum power specification might be more feasible if there is little empirical experience with a phenomenon. Moreover, this minimum power specification corresponds to the alternative hypothesis that all means other than the two extreme ones are equal to the grand mean. In this way, the problem is reduced to calculating a CI for the difference between two means (see example 1 above).

Example 8: One-Way Repeated Measures ANOVA

Power Analysis

A researcher is planning a study of changes in the level of self-esteem of offenders in a substance abuse treatment program. After completing the treatment, and at three 1-month intervals, program participants will be administered a self-esteem scale. Higher scores indicate higher levels of self-esteem. The researcher anticipates a medium effect size of $f^2 =$ 0.0625. Note that, here, *effect size is f squared;* that is, small $= (.10)^2 =$ .01, medium $= (.25)^2 = .0625$, and large $= (.40)^2 = .16$.

Table 6.10 and Figures 6.23 and 6.24 summarize a power analysis for this study in GPower. Note that GPower does not estimate sample size directly for a repeated-measures ANOVA design. Through trial and error, the researcher must identify the sample size that will yield the desired level of power.

Table 6.10

Select	Type of test	Other F-tests
	Type of power analysis	Post hoc
		Accuracy mode calculation
Input	[3]Effect size f^2	0.625
	Alpha	0.05
	N	18
	[1]Numerator df	$3 - 1 = 2$
	[2]Denominator df	$18(3 - 1) = 36$
Result	Lambda	11.2500
	Critical F	$(3,36) = 2.8663$
	Power $(1 -$ beta$)$	0.7652

[1]Numerator $df = m-1$, where m is the number of levels of the repeated factor
[2]Denominator $df = n(m-1)$, where n is the sample size
[3]Effect size $= m^*f^2/1-\rho$, where ρ is the correlation between scores at any one level of the repeated factor and any other level of the repeated fact. Note that, here, *effect size is f squared;* that is, small $= (.10)^2$, medium $= (.25)^2$, and large $= (.40)^2$. Therefore, assuming $\rho = .70$, effect size $= 3(.0625)/1 - .70 = 0.625$

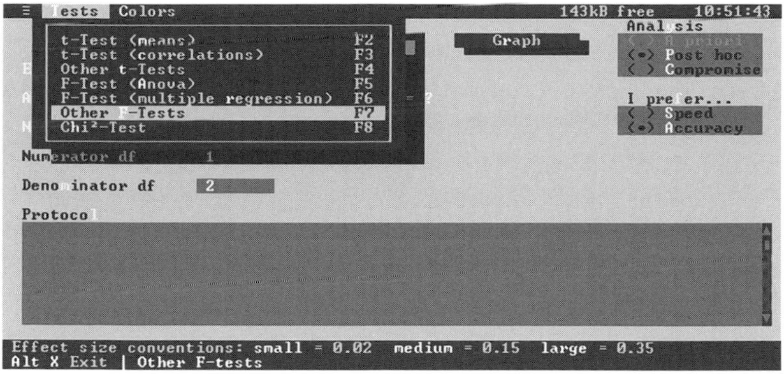

Figure 6.23. Selecting a Test in GPower

Confidence Intervals

One strategy is to compute the CI for a contrast as described previously for an ANOVA model (see example 6) and consider this CI as a conservative estimate of the true confidence interval of the ANCOVA. Another strategy is to focus on a minimum power specification; that is, focus on the difference between the largest mean and the smallest mean. Although less precise in terms of determining sample size, this minimum power specification might be more feasible if there is little

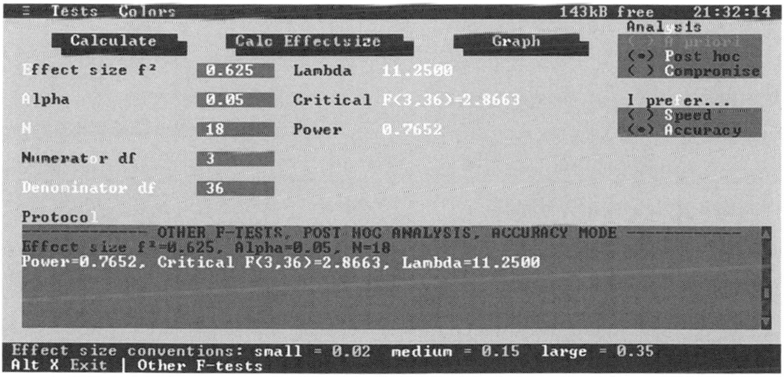

Figure 6.24. GPower Input and Results

empirical experience with a phenomenon. Moreover, this minimum power specification corresponds to the alternative hypothesis that all means other than the two extreme ones are equal to the grand mean. In this way, the problem is reduced to calculating a confidence interval for the difference between two means (see example 1).

Example 9: MANOVA

Power Analysis

A researcher is planning a study to compare levels of self-esteem and depression among Anglo, African American, and Mexican American juvenile offenders in a substance abuse treatment program. After completing the treatment, program participants will be administered a

Table 6.11

Select	Type of test	Other F-tests
	Type of power analysis	Post hoc
		Accuracy mode calculation
Input	Effect size f^2	0.15
	Alpha	0.05
	N	90
	[1]Numerator df	4
	[2]Denominator df	174
Result	Lambda	13.5000
	Critical F	$(4, 174) = 2.4236$
	Power $(1 - \text{beta})$:	0.8413

[1]Numerator degrees of freedom $= p^* \, n = 2(2) = 4$
[2]Denominator degrees of freedom $= s^* \, (N - k - p + s) = 2(45 - 3 - 2 + 2) = 174$
N is the total number of participants summed across all k groups of the design times 2 because lambda $= s(h) * N * f^2$; in this example, $N = 3 \times 15$ in each group $= 45 \times 2 = 90$
$k =$ the number of groups in the design $= 3$
$p =$ the number of dependent variables $= 2$
$n =$ using dummy coding for the 3 groups, the number of predictors for the effects to be tested $= 3 - 1 = 2$
$s =$ the smaller of either p or $n = p = 2$

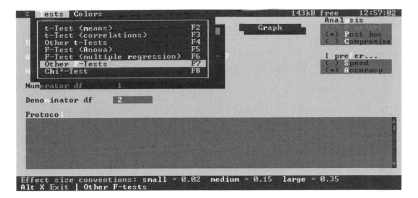

Figure 6.25. Selecting a Test in GPower

self-esteem scale, and a depression scale. Higher scores on both scales indicate higher levels of each psychological attribute. The researcher anticipates a medium effect size of $f^2 = 0.15$. Table 6.11 and Figures 6.25 and 6.26 summarize a power analysis for this study in GPower. Note that GPower does not estimate sample size directly for a MANOVA design. Through trial and error, the researcher must identify the sample size that will yield the desired level of power.

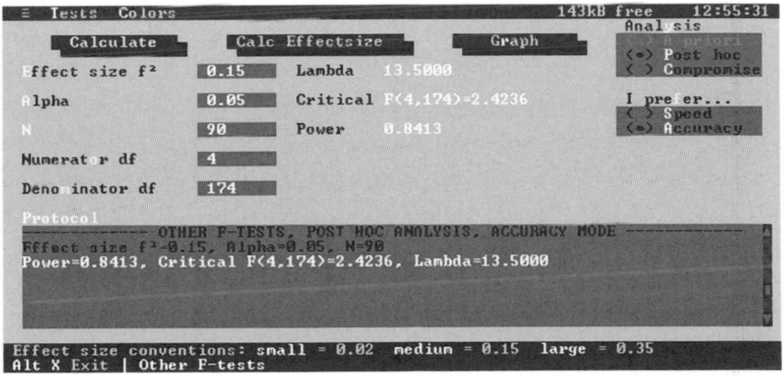

Figure 6.26. GPower Input and Results

Confidence Intervals

There are few choices. One strategy is to select a one-way model, focus on the difference between the largest mean and the smallest mean, and calculate a confidence interval around this mean difference (see example 1 for an illustration of calculating a confidence interval around a difference between two means).

Example 10: MANCOVA

Power Analysis

MANCOVA is a MANOVA in which the dependent variables (DVs) are initially adjusted for differences in one or more covariates. Resources for estimating sample size for MANCOVA are difficult to identify. One approach is to adapt the aforementioned sample size estimation strategy for MANOVA. That is, use GPower and adjust the denominator df. If k is the number of groups in the design and g is the number of covariates, then groups $= k + g$.

A researcher is planning a study to compare the levels of self-esteem and depression among Anglo, African American, and Mexican American juvenile offenders (i.e., three groups) in a substance abuse treatment program, controlling for age (i.e., one covariate). After completing the treatment, program participants will be administered a self-esteem scale and a depression scale. Higher scores on both scales indicate higher levels of each psychological attribute. The researcher anticipates a medium effect size of $f^2 = 0.15$. Table 6.12 and Figures 6.27 and 6.28 summarize a power analysis for this study in GPower. Note that GPower does not estimate sample size directly for a MANCOVA design. Through trial and error, the researcher must identify the sample size that will yield the desired level of power.

Table 6.12

Select	Type of test		Other F-tests
	Type of power analysis		Post hoc
			Accuracy mode calculation
Input	Effect size f^2		0.15
	Alpha		0.05
	N		90
	[1]Numerator df		4
	[2]Denominator df		172
Result	Lambda		13.50
	Critical F		$(4, 172) = 2.4242$
	Power $(1 - beta)$		0.8412

[1]Numerator degrees of freedom $= p^* \, n = 2(2) = 4$
[2]Denominator degrees of freedom $= s^* \, [N - (k + q) - p + s] = 2[45 - (3 + 1) -2 + 2] = 172$
N is the total number of participants summed across all k groups of the design times 2 because lambda $= s(h)^* \, N^* \, f^2$; in this example, $N = 3 \times 15$ in each group $= 45 \times 2 = 90$
$k =$ the number of groups in the design $= 3$
$q =$ the number of covariates $= 1$
$p =$ the number of dependent variables $= 2$
$n =$ using dummy coding for the 3 groups, the number of predictors for the effects to be tested $= 3 - 1 = 2$
$s =$ the smaller of either p or $n = p = 1$

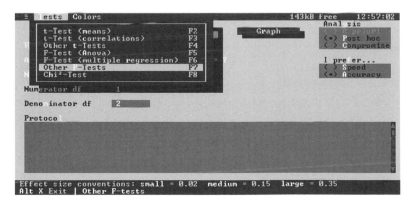

Figure 6.27. Selecting a Test in GPower

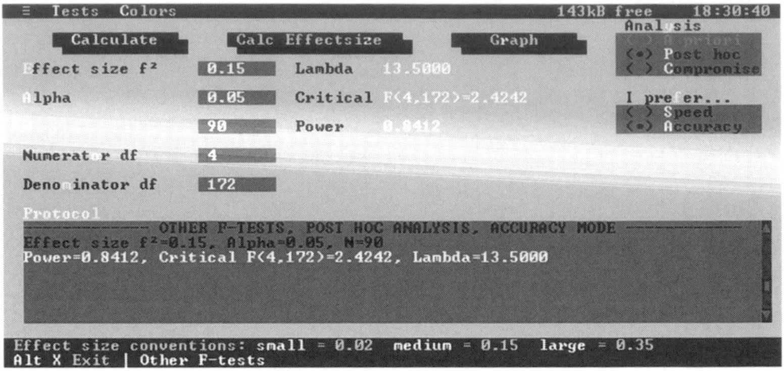

Figure 6.28. GPower Input and Results

Confidence Intervals

There are few choices. One strategy is to select a one-way model, focus on the difference between the largest mean and the smallest mean, and calculate a CI around this mean difference (see example 1 for an illustration of calculating a CI around a difference between two means).

Example 11: Repeated Measures MANOVA

Power Analysis

A researcher is planning a study of changes in the level of self-esteem of offenders in a substance abuse treatment program. After completing the treatment, and at three 1-month intervals, program participants will be administered a self-esteem scale. Higher scores indicate higher levels of self-esteem. The researcher anticipates a medium effect size of $f^2 = .0625$. Note that, here, *effect size is f squared;* that is, small $= (.10)^2 = .01$, medium $= (.25)^2 = .0625$, and large $= (.40)^2 = .16$.

Table 6.13 and Figures 6.29 and 6.30 summarize a power analysis for this study in GPower. Note that GPower does not estimate sample size

Table 6.13

Select	Type of test	Other F-tests
	Type of power analysis	Post hoc
		Accuracy mode calculation
Input	[3]Effect size f^2	0.625
	Alpha	0.05
	N	60
	[1]Numerator df	4
	[2]Denominator df	27
Result	Lambda	13.50
	Critical F	$(4,27) = 2.7278$
	Power $(1 - \text{beta})$	0.9980

[1]Numerator degrees of freedom $= p * n = 2(2) = 4$
[2]Denominator degrees of freedom $= s * (N - k - p + s) = 2(30 - 3 - 2 + 2) = 27$
[3]Effect size $= m * f^2/1 - \rho$, where ρ is the correlation between scores at any one level of the repeated factor and any other level of the repeated factor. Note that, here, *effect size* is *f squared*; that is, small $= (.10)^2$, medium $= (.25)^2$, and large $= (.40)^2$. Therefore, assuming $\rho = .70$, effect size $= 3(.0625)/1 - .70 = 0.625$.
N is the total number of participants summed across all k groups of the design times 2 because lambda $= s(h) * N * f^2$; in this example, $N = 3 \times 10$ in each group $= 30 \times 2 = 60$
$k =$ the number of groups in the design $= 3$
$p =$ the number of dependent variables $= 2$
$n =$ using dummy coding for the 3 groups, the number of predictors for the effects to be tested $= 3 - 1 = 2$
$s =$ the smaller of either p or $n = p - 2$
Note that for a repeated measures MANCOVA the numbered of groups equals k groups plus q covariates.

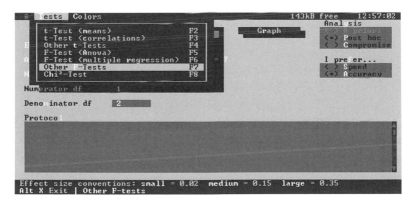

Figure 6.29. Selecting a Test in GPower

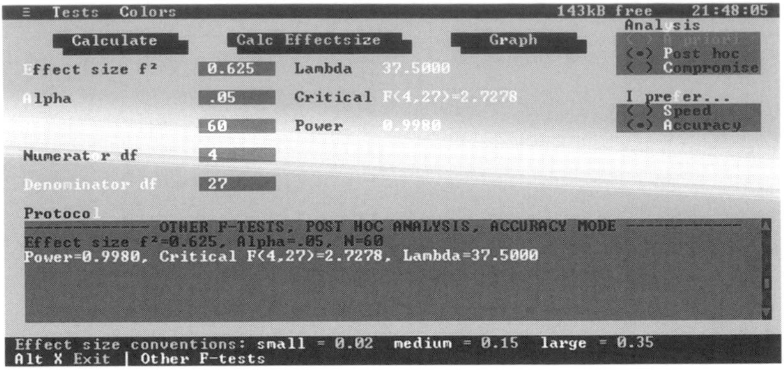

Figure 6.30. GPower Input and Results

directly for a repeated-measures MANOVA design. Through trial and error the researcher must identify the sample size that will yield the desired level of power.

Confidence Intervals

There are few choices. One strategy is to select a one-way model, focus on the difference between the largest mean and the smallest mean, and calculate a CI around this mean difference (see example 1 for an illustration of calculating a CI around a difference between two means).

Example 12: Correlation

Power Analysis

A researcher is planning to study residents of a housing development for senior citizens. The study seeks to measure the relationship between the level of physical activity of residents and the number of visitors they receive in a week. The researcher posits that there is a positive relationship between level of physical activity and number of visitors, with a

Table 6.14

Select	Type of power analysis	A priori
		Accuracy mode calculation
		One-tailed
Input	Effect size r	.5
	Alpha	0.05
	Power	0.80
Result	Delta	2.6458
	Critical t	$t(19) = 1.7291$
	Total sample size	21
	Actual power	0.8172

large effect size of $r - .50$. Table 6.14 and Figures 6.31 and 6.32 summarize a power analysis for this study in GPower.

Confidence Intervals

Assuming the aforementioned study, a researcher plans to calculate the 95% CI of an $r = 0.50$. The calculator located at http://faculty.vassar.edu/lowry/rho.html yielded the following results: $r = 0.50$, $n = 21$, 95% CI = 0.088 to 0.766 (see Figure 6.33).

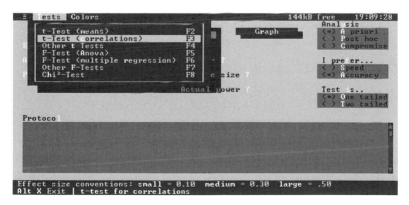

Figure 6.31. Selecting a Test in GPower

Figure 6.32. GPower Input and Results

Example 13: Regression

Power Analysis

A researcher is planning to study residents of a housing development for senior citizens. The study seeks to predict the level of physical activity of residents based on (1) the number of visitors they receive in a week, (2) their ages, and (3) their years of education. The researcher posits that there is a positive relationship between level of physical activity, number of visitors, age, and years of education, with a large effect size of $f^2 = .35$. Table 6.15 and Figures 6.34 and 6.35 summarize a power analysis for this study in Gpower.

Confidence Intervals

Assuming the aforementioned study, a researcher plans to calculate the 95% CI of an $R^2 = 0.60$. The calculator at http://www.danielsoper.com/statcalc/calc28.aspx yields the following output: 95% CI = 0.4203 to 0.7797 (see Figures 6.36 and 6.37).

VassarStats

The Confidence Interval of rho

The correlation, r, observed within a sample of XY values can be taken as an estimate of rho, the correlation that exists within the general population of bivariate values from which the sample is randomly drawn. This page will calculate the 0.95 and 0.99 confidence intervals for rho, based on the Fisher r-to-z transformation.

For the notation used here, r = the Pearson product-moment correlation coefficient observed within the sample and n = the number of paired XY observations on which the sample r is based. For purposes of this calculation, the value of n must be equal to or greater than 4.

To perform the calculations, enter the values of r and n in the designated places, then click the «Calculate» button. Note that the confidence interval of rho is symmetrical around the observed r only with large values of n.

r = 50
n = 21

Reset
Calculate

0.95 and 0.99 Confidence Intervals of rho

	Lower Limit	Upper Limit
0.95	0.088	0.766
0.99	-0.057	0.819

Home Click this link only if you did not arrive here via the VassarStats main page.

Figure 6.33. VassarStats Input and Results

Table 6.15

Select	Type of power analysis	A priori Accuracy mode calculation
	Hypothesis	Global
Input	Effect size f^2	.35
	Alpha	0.05
	Power	0.80
	Predictors	3
Result	Lambda	2.6458
	Critical t	$F(13,32) = 2.9011$
	Total sample size	36
	Actual power	0.8095

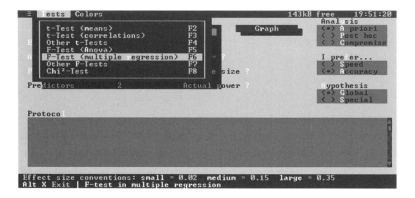

Figure 6.34. Selecting a Test in GPower

Figure 6.35. GPower Input and Results

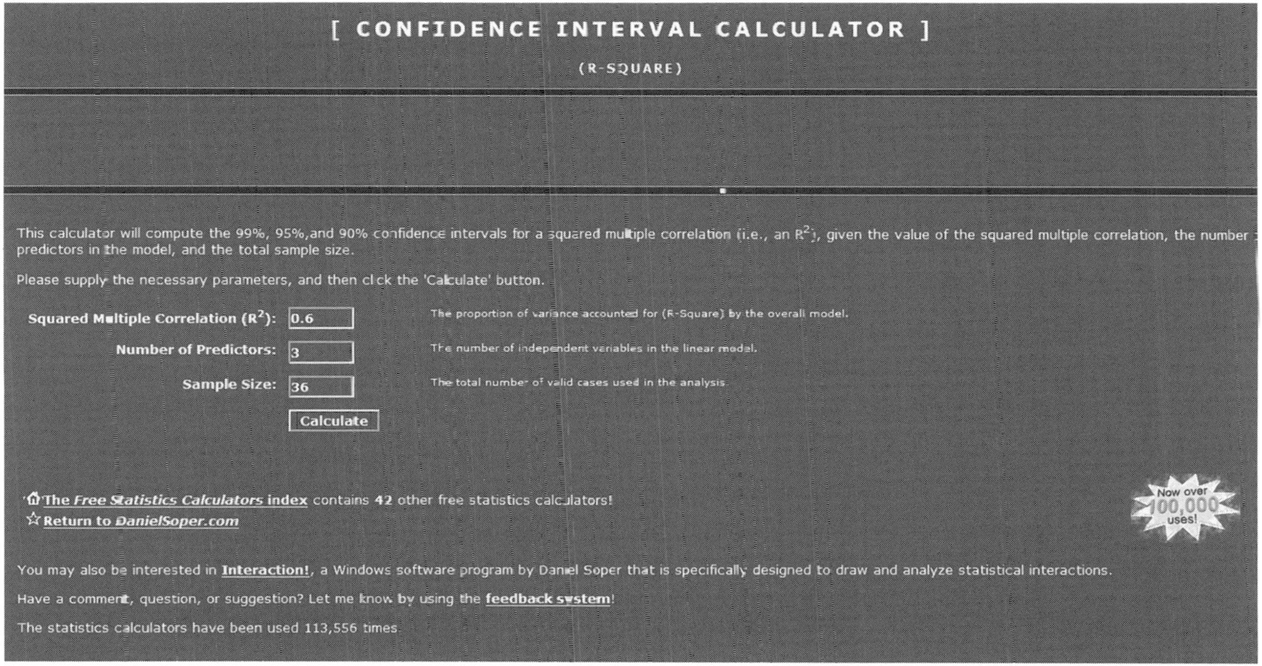

[CONFIDENCE INTERVAL CALCULATOR]

(R-SQUARE)

This calculator will compute the 99%, 95%, and 90% confidence intervals for a squared multiple correlation (i.e., an R^2_s), given the value of the squared multiple correlation, the number of predictors in the model, and the total sample size.

Please supply the necessary parameters, and then click the 'Calculate' button.

Squared Multiple Correlation (R^2): `0.6`   The proportion of variance accounted for (R-Square) by the overall model.

Number of Predictors: `3`   The number of independent variables in the linear model.

Sample Size: `36`   The total number of valid cases used in the analysis

`Calculate`

The *Free Statistics Calculators* index contains **42** other free statistics calculators!
☆ **Return to** *DanielSoper.com*

You may also be interested in **Interaction!**, a Windows software program by Daniel Soper that is specifically designed to draw and analyze statistical interactions.

Have a comment, question, or suggestion? Let me know, by using the **feedback system**!

The statistics calculators have been used 113,556 times

Figure 6.36. Input from http://www.danielsoper.com

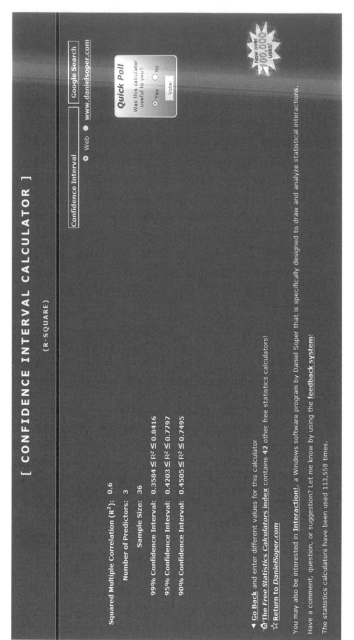

Figure 6.37. Output from http://www.danielsoper.com

Example 14: Discriminant Function Analysis (DFA)

Power Analysis

Computationally similar to MANOVA, all assumptions for MANOVA apply to discriminant function analysis (DFA). Therefore, sample size can be determined with the aforementioned MANOVA strategies. The principal difference between MANOVA and DFA is the labeling of the dependent and independent variables (Stevens, 2002). Researchers will temporarily need to reconceptualize the DFA model as a MANOVA model by reversing the IVs and the DV. That is, instead of asking: What is the relationship between the IVs and group membership? ask: What characteristics best distinguish groups A and B?

For example, a researcher is planning a study to compare agencies serving homeless people who are less than 20 years old (type A) with agencies serving homeless people who are more than 20 years old (type B). Here, the research question for a DFA is what factors (i.e., size of annual budget, religious versus nonsectarian mission, type of services provided, and the number of professionally trained social workers employed) distinguish type A agencies with type B agencies. The researcher wishes to perform a power analysis to determine sample size and, consequently, she temporarily reframes the question for a MANOVA as follows: What is the relationship between size of annual budget, religious versus nonsectarian mission, type of services provided, and the number of professionally trained social workers employed and type A versus type B group membership? Table 6.16 and Figures 6.38 and 6.39 summarize her power analysis in Power Analysis and Sample Size (PASS):

Table 6.16

Select		PASS
		Means
		Multivariate
		Hotelling's T-squared (because this design contains two groups; for three or more groups, select MANOVA)
Input	Solve for	N or N_1
	Groups	2
	Response variables	3
	Mean differences	Ability to detect small differences $= .50$
	K	1
	N_1	0
	Alpha	0.05
	N_2	Use R
	Beta	0.20
	R	1.0
Result		$N_1 = N_2 = 18$; therefore $N = 18$ in each group

Example 15: Logistic Regression

Power Analysis

A researcher plans a study to compare the decision-making styles of a randomly selected group of supervisors in Agency A with employees' perceptions of being burned out. Supervisors would be categorized as either "democratic" or "autocratic" based on a standardized scale score. Workers would be categorized as either being "burned out" or "not burned out" based on a standardized scale score. The researcher's model includes two covariates: age and race of employees. The researcher anticipates a medium effect size of $d = 0.5$.

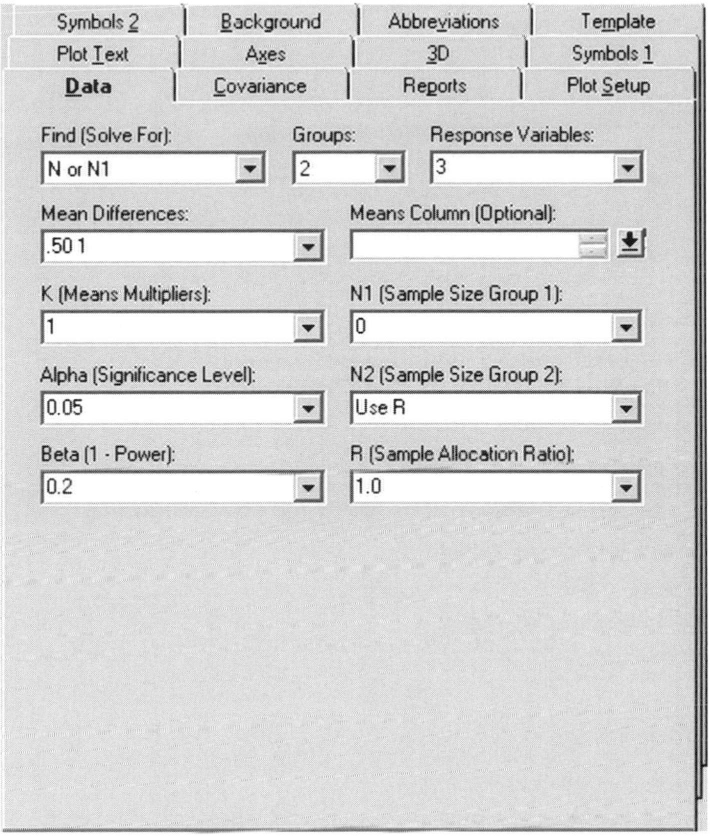

Figure 6.38.   PASS Input

Hsieh, Bloch, and Larsen (1998) and Vaeth and Skovlund (2004) recommended modifying a two-sample calculation (i.e., t-test; see example 1 for an illustration) by a "variance inflation factor" such as $N_m = N_1/(1 - p^2)$, where N_1 and N_m are the required sample sizes with 1 and m covariates, respectively, and p^2 is the multiple correlation coefficient between the variable of interest (supervisory style) and the remaining $m - 1$ covariates. Table 6.17 summarizes a power analysis for this study in GPower.

Hotelling's T-Squared Power Analysis

Page/Date/Time   1   12/31/2006 11:51:48 PM

Numeric Results

Power	N1	N2	Multiply Means By (K)	Alpha	Beta	Effect Size	Number of Y's (DF1)	DF2
0.8017	18	18	1.0000	0.0500	0.2000	1.17	3	32

References
Rencher, Alvin C. 1998. Multivariate Statistical Inference and Applications. John Wiley. New York, New York.

Report Definitions
Power is the probability of rejecting a false null hypothesis. Note that Power = 1 - Beta.
N1 and N2 are the sample sizes of the two groups.
K is a constant by which all means are multiplied.
Alpha is the probability of rejecting a true null hypothesis.
Beta is the probability of accepting a false null hypothesis. Note that Beta = 1 - Power.
Effect Size is a standardized version of T2 under the alternative hypothesis.
DF1 is the first degrees of freedom of T2. It is the number of response variables.
DF2 is the second degrees of freedom of T2.

Summary Statements
Sample sizes of 18 in group one and 18 in group two achieve 80% power to detect an effect size of 1.17 which represents the differences between the group means of the 3 response variables, adjusted by the variance-covariance matrix. The two-sample Hotelling's T-squared test statistic is used with a significance level of 0.0500.

Chart Section

N1 vs K with Alpha=0.05 Power=0.80 N2=N1

Figure 6.39. PASS Results

The squared multiple correlation coefficient between the covariate of interest (supervisory style) and the other two covariates (age and race) was estimated to be .4. Therefore, the final sample size is $102/(1-.4^2) = 102/(1-.16) = 102/.84 = 121$ (see Figures 6.40 and 6.41).

Confidence Intervals

No practical strategies have emerged in the literature.

Table 6.17

Select	t-test (means)	
	Type of power analysis	A priori
	Type of test	t-test (means), two-tailed
		Accuracy mode calculation
Input	Effect size d	0.5
		Note that to calculate the effect size from mean A, mean B, and the pooled standard deviation, click "Calc d," insert the means and the standard deviation, and click "Calc & Copy."
	Alpha	.05
	Power (1 – beta)	.8
Click Calculate		
Result	Total sample size	102
	Actual power	.8059
	Critical t	1.6602
	Delta	Noncentrality parameter = 2.5249

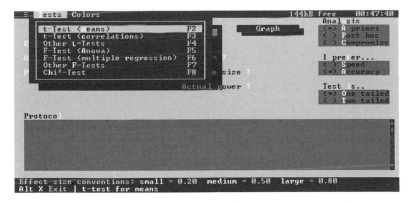

Figure 6.40. Selecting a Test in GPower

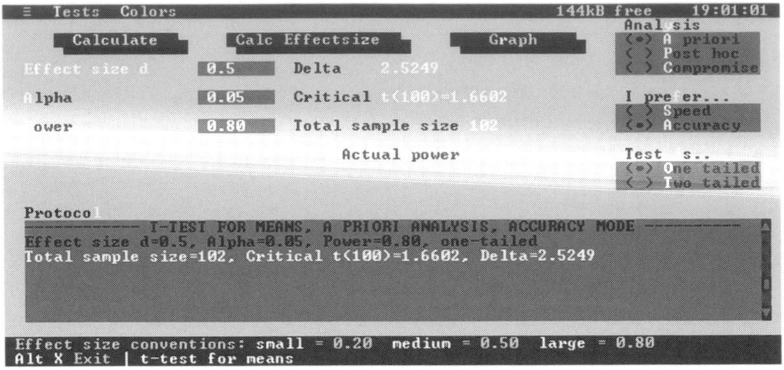

Figure 6.41. GPower Input and Results

Example 16: Cox Regression

Power Analysis

A study is planned to compare the decision-making styles of a randomly selected group of supervisors in Agency A and the time to first promotion of employees that they have supervised. Supervisors were categorized as either "democratic" or "autocratic" based on a standardized scale score.

When comparing two groups using a Cox regression model, the sample size can be obtained from the formula for the log-rank test (Hsieh et al., 1998; Vaeth & Skovlund, 2004). The log-rank test computes a P value that answers this question: If the two populations have identical survival curves overall, what is the chance that random sampling of participants would lead to as big a difference in survival (or bigger) as you observed (Hsieh, Lavori, Cohen, & Feussner, 2003)? If the p-value is small ($< .05$), then the null hypothesis that the two populations have identical survival characteristics is rejected (Cox & Oakes, 2001). After calculating the sample size required for a univariate

Table 6.18

Select	Goal	Survival
	Number of groups	Two
	Analysis method	Test
Input	Alpha	.05
	One- or two-sided test	One
	Group 1 proportion	0.90
	Group 2 proportion	0.50
	Hazard ratio	0.152
	Power (%)	80
	Click on blank cell adjacent to n to calculate	
Result	N per group:	20
	Total number of events required	7

analysis to study the effect of X_1 on endpoint Y, inflate the sample size as described for logistic regression. Table 6.18 summarizes a power analysis for this study in nQuery Advisor.

The squared multiple correlation coefficient between the covariate of interest (supervisory style) and the other two covariates (age and race) was estimated to be .4. Therefore, the final sample size is $40/(1 - .4^2) = 40/(1 - .16) = 40/.84 = 48$ (see Figures 6.42 and 6.43).

Confidence Intervals

No practical strategies have emerged in the literature.

Example 17: Structural Equation Modeling (SEM)

Power Analysis

A study is planned to examine the relationship between factors that influence postadoption service utilization and positive adoption

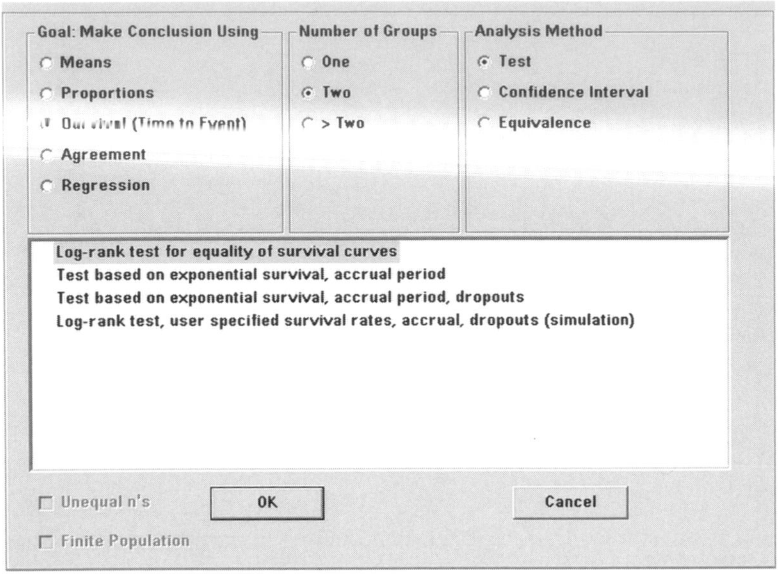

Figure 6.42. Selecting a Test in nQuery Advisor

	1	2	3
Test significance level, α	0.050		
1 or 2 sided test?	1		
Group 1 proportion π_1 at time t	0.900		
Group 2 proportion π_2 at time t	0.500		
Hazard ratio, $h=\ln(\pi_1) / \ln(\pi_2)$	0.152		
Power (%)	80		
n per group	20		
Total number of events required, E	7		

Figure 6.43. nQuery Advisor Results

outcomes. Specifically, the study tests a model that links (1) factors influencing the utilization of postadoption services (parents' perceptions of self-efficacy, relationship satisfaction between parents, knowledge of available postadoption services, and attitudes toward adoption) with (2) service utilization (two groups, used versus did not use postadoption services), and (3) positive adoption outcomes (satisfaction with parenting and satisfaction with adoption agency).

As discussed in chapter 2, structural equation modeling (SEM) does not use raw data. Instead, in SEM the variance (or covariance) matrix is used. The number of observations in SEM is defined as the number of covariances in the matrix rather than the number of cases in a data set. The number of observations or covariances in SEM can be calculated as follows: $v(v+1)/2$, where $v = $ the number of variables in the model. In the current model, there are seven variables (i.e., the four instruments measuring factors influencing the utilization of postadoption service, the two instruments measuring adoption outcomes, and one measure of service utilization). Therefore, the number of variables in this example is $7(7+1)/2$, or 23.

This example determines sample size by following the approach proposed by MacCallum, Browne, and Sugawara (1996), which was described in chapter 2. This approach uses the root mean square error of approximation to calculate power (RMSEA; see chapter 2, endnote 9; Browne & Cudeck, 1993; Hu & Bentler, 1999; Steiger, 1990). This index weighs absolute fit, which declines whenever a parameter is removed from the model, against model complexity, such that the benefits of parsimony are considered along with fit (Steiger, 2000). Models fitting with RMSEA < .05 are usually considered as having a "close" fit, .05 to .08 as having a "fair" fit, .08 to .10 as having a "mediocre" fit, and above .10 as having a "poor" fit (MacCallum et al., 1996).

A program called NIESEM performs power analysis according to the approach proposed by MacCallum et al. (1996). NIESEM is free and available for download from http://rubens.its.unimelb.edu.au/~dudgeon/. Table 6.19 and Figures 6.44 and 6.45 summarize a power analysis for this study in NIESEM.

Table 6.19

Input	Power calculations
	estimate N for a given power
	power equals 0.80
	the null hypothesized RMSEA value = 0.00
	the alternative hypothesized RMSEA value = 0.05
	the chosen alpha level = 0.05
	the degrees of freedom (df) of the model = $[7(7+1)]/2 = 28$; note that $df = p(p + 1)/2$, where there are p observed variables in the model
	the number of groups in the model = 2
Result	Estimated sample size = 684

Confidence Intervals

MacCallum et al. (1996) suggested that the possibility of a "good" fit is indicated by a CI that include values between 0 and .05. Table 6.20 summarizes a power analysis for this study in NIESEM:

Because NIESEM yields the value of .0000 to .0553 for the 95% CI around RMSEA and because this interval includes values between 0 and .05, it suggests the possibility of good fit (MacCallum et al., 1996).

```
SEM Power Analysis Submenu:
============================
                        [a]  Estimate power for given N
                        [b]  Estimate N for given power

                        [z]  Return ot main menu

Select a menu item letter:
```

Figure 6.44. NIESEM Input

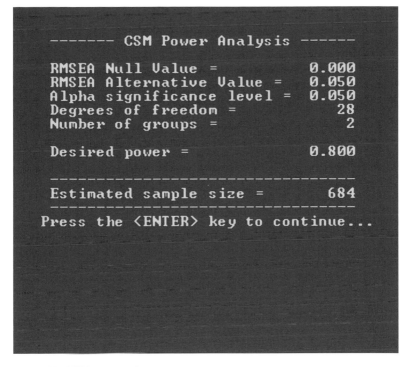

Figure 6.45. NTF.SEM Results

Table 6.20

Input	RMSEA & ECVI calculations
	the discrepancy function value = .05
	degrees of freedom = 28
	sample size for all groups combined = 684
	the number of sample groups = 2
	required confidence interval percentage = 95
	the null approximate fit RMSEA test value = .05
	ML (maximum likelihood estimate) = yes
	the number of observed variables used in the model = 7
	Parameters entered directly = no
Result	RMSEA value is: 0.0253; 95% CI 0.0000 to 0.0553

Through trial and error, the researcher might wish to adjust sample size until the minimum sample size necessary for a 95% CI around RMSEA that includes values between 0 and .05 is identified (see Figures 6.46 and 6.47).

Example 18: Multilevel Analysis

Power Analysis

A researcher is planning a study of a state-sponsored domestic violence treatment program. The program will be offered at four locations in each of the five regions across the state. Sites will be selected using stratified random sampling to balance the number of observations across regions. Participants will be randomly assigned to a treatment group or a waiting list for the program. A third group, referred to here as a comparison group, will consist of randomly selected participants in an existing counseling program for couples. Program effectiveness will be evaluated by comparing the scores of the treatment, control, and comparison groups on a conflict resolution skill scale. The scale measures

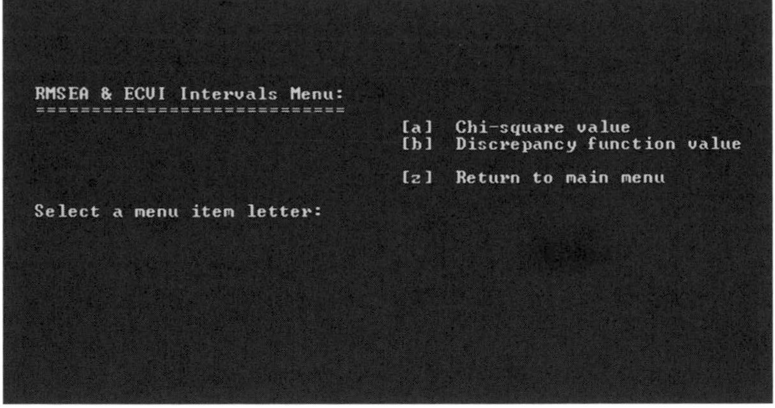

```
RMSEA & ECUI Intervals Menu:
==============================
                              [a]  Chi-square value
                              [b]  Discrepancy function value

                              [z]  Return to main menu

Select a menu item letter:
```

Figure 6.46. NIESEM Input

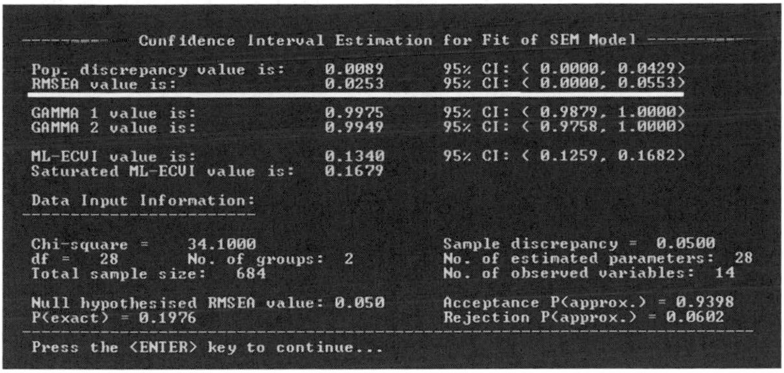

```
--------- Confidence Interval Estimation for Fit of SEM Model ---------

Pop. discrepancy value is:      0.0089      95% CI: ( 0.0000, 0.0429)
RMSEA value is:                 0.0253      95% CI: ( 0.0000, 0.0553)

GAMMA 1 value is:               0.9975      95% CI: ( 0.9879, 1.0000)
GAMMA 2 value is:               0.9949      95% CI: ( 0.9758, 1.0000)

ML-ECVI value is:               0.1340      95% CI: ( 0.1259, 0.1682)
Saturated ML-ECVI value is:     0.1679

Data Input Information:
-----------------------

Chi-square =    34.1000                     Sample discrepancy =   0.0500
df =   28       No. of groups:  2           No. of estimated parameters:  28
Total sample size:   684                    No. of observed variables:  14

Null hypothesised RMSEA value: 0.050        Acceptance P(approx.) = 0.9398
P(exact) = 0.1976                           Rejection P(approx.) = 0.0602
--------------------------------------------------------------------------
Press the <ENTER> key to continue...
```

Figure 6.47. NIESEM Input

a person's ability to suggest solutions to interpersonal conflicts that consider other people's perspectives. Scores range from 0 to 100, with 55 considered "moderate" and 45 considered "low."

Previous research indicates that the scale has a mean of 50 and an $SD = 15$. Assuming a moderate effect of $f = .25$, one-tailed alpha level = .05, and power = .08, GPower was used to determine sample size. In GPower, select *F*-test (ANOVA). Enter effect size, alpha, and power; indicate that test is one-tailed; and click "calculate." See example 6 for screenshots of ANOVA in GPower. Given these specifications, GPower indicated the need for a sample size of 159 (approximately 53 participants in each group) in each region.

Confidence Intervals

As discussed in chapter 2, determining the sample size for an ANOVA design is usually difficult because of the need to specify all of the treatment means and standard deviations. An alternative is to focus on the difference between the largest mean and the smallest mean. Although less precise in terms of determining sample size, this minimum power specification might be more feasible if there is little empirical experience with a phenomenon. Moreover, this minimum power specification corresponds to the alternative hypothesis that all means other than the two extreme ones are equal to the grand mean. In this way, the problem is reduced to calculating a confidence interval for the difference between two means. Assuming equal group sizes equal to 53 and an *SD* of 15, the calculator at http://graphpad.com/quickcalcs/ErrorProp1.cfm was used to compute the 95% CI around the difference between the largest (55) and the smallest (45) expected group means. The calculator yielded the following output: 95% CI $= -15.78$ to -4.22. Because the largest expected difference among the three groups is 10, the researcher needs to decide whether this is an acceptable level of precision. This CI seems large, as the interval is equal to largest expected difference among the three groups. However, it is not unusual to have large CIs associated with sample size associated with a conventionally acceptable level of power, such as .80.

Multilevel Analysis

Because stratified sampling is planned, sample size must be adjusted for design effect. As discussed in chapter 2, the design effect provides a correction for the loss of sampling efficiency, resulting from the use of stratified sampling as opposed to simple random sampling. Thus design effect may be simply interpreted as the factor by which the sample size for a stratified sample would have to be increased in order to produce estimates with the same precision as a simple random sample.

The magnitude of design effect depends on two factors: (1) the degree of similarity or homogeneity of elements within strata and (2) the number of sample elements to be taken from each stratum. The initial factor, the homogeneity of elements within strata, is a population characteristic over which the survey taker has no control. Prior methodological research indicates that most population characteristics tend to cluster and that it is prudent to assume that some degree of homogeneity within strata exists. The second parameter, the number of elementary units chosen per strata, is largely within the control of the survey taker and is an important consideration in the sample design for any survey.

The design effect is approximately equal to $1 +$ (average stratum size -1) $\times$ intra correlation coefficient (ICC). Muthen and Satorra

(1995) view a design effect of 2 as small. Generally, design effects range from 1 to 3, but higher values are possible, and a reasonable approach is to use a design effect of 2 or 3 (Lê & Verma, 1997).

Final sample size, therefore, is calculated as $160 \times 2 = 320$ (approximately 107 in each group statewide). Note that a sample size of 160 is used here instead of 159 as calculated previously for power and CI estimation to facilitate calculations in this example. Assuming equal sample across the four agencies in each region, $N = 6$ participants in each of the three groups in each agency should provide ample power for the study. These calculations are summarized as follows: 6×3 groups $= 18$; 18×4 agencies in each region $= 64$; 64×5 regions $= 320$ statewide.

Example 19: CI Around an Effect Size

A researcher is planning a study of a state-sponsored domestic violence treatment program. The program will be offered at four locations in each of the five regions across the state. Sites will be selected using stratified random sampling to balance the number of observations across regions. Participants will be randomly assigned to a treatment group or a waiting list for the program. A third group, referred to here as a comparison group, consisted of randomly selected participants in an existing counseling program for couples. Program effectiveness would be evaluated by comparing the scores of the treatment, control, and comparison groups on a conflict resolution skill scale. The scale measures a person's ability to suggest solutions to interpersonal conflicts that consider other people's perspectives. Scores range from 0 to 100, with 55 considered "moderate" and 45 considered "low."

In addition to a CI around the difference between two means, the researcher is interested in evaluating the CI around the effect size d. As discussed in chapter 2, the appropriate probability distribution is noncentral t; that is, values of t if the null hypothesis of no difference between the means is false. In the case of the noncentral t, there are an infinite number of such distributions, one for every possible value of the parameter (effect size), making tables of little value.

To calculate the CI around d, download NoncT.sav (necessary data file) and T-d-2samples.sps (syntax file) from http://core.ecu.edu/psyc/wuenschk/SPSS/SPSS-Programs.htm.

Assuming an expected difference of 10 and a pooled SD of 15, d equals $10/15 = .67$. The 95% CI around d is calculated as follows:

1. Run an independent-samples t-test. There does not seem to be a consensus about whether to use a "separate variances" or a "pooled" t and df when computing the CI around d with equal group sizes (cf. Zimmerman, 2004). The separate-variance t-test tends to be more conservative and is used in this example. The following calculator will tell you the Student t-value, given the probability and the degrees of freedom: http://www.danielsoper.com/statcalc/calc10.aspx. For $p = .05$, $df = 104$, t-value $= 1.98$.
2. Open NoncT.sav, which consists of one row of data with 13 variables.
3. In the column labeled $tval$, enter the obtained t-value of 1.98.
4. In the df column, enter the degrees of freedom of 104.
5. In the $conf$ column, enter 0.95 for a 95% CI.
6. In the n_1 (size of group 1) column, enter 53.
7. In the n_2 (size of group 2) column, enter 53.
8. Open the T-D-2sample.sps file.
9. On the command bar, click Run and select "All."

As a result of running the preceding syntax, Nonct.sav now contains the lower limit of the confidence interval ($lowd$ column) and the upper limit of the CI ($highd$ column). The 95% CI of d for this example is $-.0007$ to $.7680$. As discussed in chapter 3, CIs around effect sizes tend to be wider than CIs around nonstandardized values (i.e., the difference between two means). In part, wider CIs for effect sizes can result from combining information about raw effects (i.e., mean differences) and variation (Lenth, 2001; Steiger, 2004).

Appendix

Annotated Bibliography of Readings and Other Resources

Books and Journal Articles

Chapter 1. Basic Terms and Concepts

Adcock, C. J. (1997). Sample size determination. A review. *The Statistician,* 46(2), 261–283.

> This is a discussion of frequentist and Bayesian methods of sample size determination. Frequentist methods specify a null and alternative hypothesis for the parameter of interest and then find the sample size by controlling both size and power. These methods often need to use prior information but cannot allow for the uncertainty that is associated with it. By contrast, the Bayesian approach offers a wide variety of techniques, all of which offer the ability to deal with uncertainty associated with prior information.

Cochran, W. G. (1977). *Sampling techniques.* New York: Wiley.

> This is a classic textbook on the theory of sample surveys, that is, selection methods, sample size estimation, and analysis of data. A

calculus background and a first course in mathematical statistics are recommended to fully comprehend discussion in this book.

Cuddeback, G., Wilson, E., Orme, J. G., & Combs-Orme, T. (2004). Detecting and statistically correcting sample selection bias. *Journal of Social Service Research*, *30*(3), 19–33.

Typically, social work researchers use bivariate tests to detect selection bias (e.g., χ^2 to compare the races of participants and nonparticipants). Occasionally multiple regression methods are used (e.g., logistic regression with participation/nonparticipation as the dependent variable). Neither of these methods can be used to correct substantive results for selection bias. Sample selection models are a well-developed class of econometric models that can be used to detect and correct for selection bias, but these are rarely used in social work research. This article argues that sample selection models can help further social work research by providing researchers with methods of detecting and correcting sample selection bias.

Fink, A. (2002). *How to sample in surveys* (Volume 7). Thousand Oaks, CA: Sage Publications.

This book covers probability and nonprobability sampling methods, calculating response rates, and dealing with sampling error and also treats determining sample size and statistical power.

Hoyle, R. H. (1999). *Statistical strategies for small sample research*. Thousand Oaks, CA: Sage Publications.

This book describes and illustrates statistical strategies that are appropriate for analyzing data from small samples of fewer than 150 cases. It covers such topics as ways to increase power when sample size cannot be increased; strategies for computing effect sizes and combining effect sizes across studies; how to hypothesis test using bootstrapping; and methods for pooling effect size indicators from single-case studies.

Huberty, C. (1993). Historical origins of statistical testing practices: The treatment of Fisher versus Neyman-Pearson views in textbooks. *Journal of Experimental Education, 61,* 317–333.

Twenty-eight books published from 1910 to 1949, 19 books published from 1990 to 1992, plus 5 multiple-edition books are reviewed in terms of presentations of coverage of the *p*-value (i.e., Fisher) and fixed-alpha (i.e., Neyman-Pearson) approaches to statistical testing. Also of interest in the review are issues and concerns related to the practice and teaching of statistical testing: (a) levels of significance, (b) importance of effects, (c) statistical power and sample size, and (d) multiple testing. The author concludes that the textbook presentations and teaching practices do not always accurately reflect the views of Fisher and Neyman-Pearson.

Kish, L. (1965). *Survey sampling.* New York: Wiley.

This is a classic textbook on the applied aspects of sample surveys, particularly in design and analysis. It contains discussion of the details of multistage sampling that are not discussed in other books and includes practical guidelines.

Peterson, R. S., Smith, B. D., & Martorana, P. V. (2006). Choosing between a rock and a hard place when data are scarce and questions important: A reply to Hooenbeck, DeRue, and Mannor (2006). *Journal of Applied Psychology, 9* (1), 6–8.

This article discusses the dilemmas faced in conducting empirical research in a nascent area and suggests that theory development in such a situation can be well served by studies that use alternative or new methods with small samples. Theory development scholarship using small-sample research methods (e.g., case studies and

Q-sorting from archival sources) can be useful for stimulating ideas, theory, and research programs that can be tested with large-sample quantitative research.

Chapter 2. Statistical Power Analysis

Algina, J., & Olejnik, S. (2000). Determining sample size for accurate estimation of the squared multiple correlation coefficient. *Multivariate Behavioral Research, 35*(1), 119–137.

This article focuses on the squared multiple correlation coefficient and presents regression equations that permit determination of sample size for estimating this parameter for up to 20 predictor variables. A comparison of the sample sizes reported here with those needed to test the hypothesis of no relationship between the predictor and criterion variables demonstrates the need for researchers to consider the purpose of their research and what is to be reported when determining the sample size for the study.

Algina, J., & Olejnik, S. (2003). Sample size tables for correlation analysis with applications in partial correlation and multiple regression analysis. *Multivariate Behavioral Research, 38* (3), 309–323.

Tables for selecting sample size in correlation studies are presented. Applications of the tables in partial correlation and multiple regression analyses are discussed. SAS and SPSS computer programs are provided to permit researchers to select sample size for levels of accuracy, for probabilities, for parameter values, and for Type I error rates other than those used in constructing the tables.

Campbell, M. J, Julious, S. A., & Altman, D. G. (1995). Estimating sample sizes for binary, ordered categorical and continuous outcomes in two group comparisons. *British Medical Journal, 311*, 1145–1148.

The authors outline strategies for calculating sample sizes in two-group studies for binary, ordered categorical, and continuous outcomes. Formulas and worked examples are provided. Maximum power is usually achieved by having equal numbers in the two groups. However, this is not always possible, and calculations for unequal group sizes are suggested.

Cohen, J. (1988). *Statistical power analysis for the behavioral sciences* (2nd ed.). Hillsdale, NJ: Erlbaum.

This is the classic reference for statistical power analysis.

D'Amico, E. J., Neilands T. B., & Zambarano, R. (2001). Power analysis for multivariate and repeated measures designs: A flexible approach using the SPSS MANOVA procedure. *Behavior Research Methods, Instruments, and Computers, 33*(4), 479–484.

This article presents an SPSS procedure that can be used for calculating power for univariate, multivariate, and repeated-measures models with and without time-varying and time-constant covariates. Three examples provide a framework for calculating power via this method: an ANCOVA, a MANOVA, and a repeated-measures ANOVA with two or more groups. The benefits and limitations of this procedure are discussed.

Gastonis, C., & Sampson, A. R. (1989). Multiple correlation: Exact power and sample size calculations. *Psychological Bulletin, 106*(3), 516–524.

This article discusses power and sample size calculations for observational studies in which the values of the independent variables cannot be fixed in advance but are themselves outcomes of the study. It reviews the mathematical framework applicable when a multivariate normal distribution can be assumed and describes a method for calculating exact power and sample sizes using a series expansion for the distribution of the multiple correlation coefficient. A table of exact sample sizes for level .05 tests is provided. Approximations to the exact power are discussed, most notably those of Cohen (1977). A rigorous justification of Cohen's approximations is given. Comparisons with exact answers show that the approximations are accurate in many situations of practical interest.

Hancock, G. R., & Freeman, M. J. (2001). Power and sample size for the root mean square error of approximation test of not close fit in structural equation modeling. *Educational and Psychological Measurement, 61*(5), 741–758.

The authors provide power and sample size tables and interpolation strategies associated with the root mean square error of approximation (RMSEA) test of not close fit under standard assumed conditions. It is hoped that researchers conducting structural equation modeling will be better informed as to power limitations when testing a model given a particular available sample size, or, better yet, that they will heed the sample size recommendations contained herein when planning their study to ensure the most accurate assessment of the degree of close fit between data and model.

Howell, D. C. (2007). *Statistical methods for psychology* (6th ed.). Belmont, CA: Wadsworth.

This book is an excellent beginning to intermediate level text. Chapter 8 presents a very readable introduction to power analysis and provides tables for estimating power of *d* (see "Appendix Power" at http://www.uvm.edu/~dhowell/gradstat/psych340/Lectures/Power/power.html).

MacCallum, R. C., Browne, M. W., & Sugawara, H. M. (1996). Power analysis and determination of sample size for covariance structure modeling. *Psychological Methods, 1*(2), 130–149.

This article presents a framework for hypothesis testing and power analysis in the assessment of fit of covariance structure models. It emphasizes the value of confidence intervals for fit indices and stresses the relationship of confidence intervals to a framework for hypothesis testing. The approach allows for testing null hypotheses of not-good fit, reversing the role of the null hypothesis in conventional tests of model fit so that a significant result provides strong support for good fit. The approach also allows for direct estimation of power, where effect size is defined in terms of a null and alternative value of the root-mean-square error of approximation fit index (RMSEA). It is also feasible to determine minimum sample size required to achieve a given level of power for any test of fit in this framework. Computer programs and examples are provided for power analyses and calculation of minimum sample sizes.

Muller, K. E., LaVange, L. M., Ramey, S. L., & Ramey, C. T. (1992). Power calculations for general linear multivariate models including repeated measures applications. *Journal of the American Statistical Association, 87,* 1209–1226.

The authors use the development of a research proposal to discuss power analysis. Procedures described include MANOVA, ANOVA, and multiple regression.

Murphy, K., & Myors, B. (2003) *Statistical power analysis: A simple and general model for traditional and modern hypothesis tests* (2nd ed.). Mahwah, NJ: Erlbaum.

This book presents a method for reducing power analysis to the *F* distribution.

Whitley, E., & Ball, J. (2002). Statistics review 4: Sample size calculations. *Critical Care, 6,* 335–341.

This article provides a worked example of sample size calculation for a difference between proportions with a nomogram, which is a two-dimensional diagram designed to allow the approximate graphical computation of power and sample size.

Chapter 3. Confidence Intervals: Measures of Precision

Algina, J., & Keselman, H. J. (2003). Approximate confidence intervals for effect sizes. *Educational and Psychological Measurement, 63* (4), 537–553.

This article defines an approximate confidence interval for effect size in correlated (repeated-measures) groups designs. The authors found that their method was much more accurate than the interval presented and acknowledged to be approximate by Bird (2002). That is, the coverage probability over all the conditions investigated was very close to the theoretical .95 value. By contrast, Bird's interval could have coverage probability that was substantially below .95. In addition, the authors' interval was less likely than Bird's method to present an overly optimistic portrayal of the effect. They also examined the operating characteristics of the Bird (2002) interval for effect size in an independent-groups design and found that, although it is fairly accurate in its approximation of coverage probability, the accuracy of the approximation does vary with the magnitude of the population effect size.

Algina, J., & Moulder, B. C. (2001). Sample sizes for confidence intervals on the increase in the squared multiple correlation coefficient. *Educational and Psychological Measurement, 61*(4), 633–649.

The increase in the squared multiple correlation coefficient associated with a variable in a regression equation is a commonly used measure of importance in regression analysis. The article investigates the probability that an asymptotic confidence interval will include R^2.

Bird, K. D. (2002). Confidence intervals for effect sizes in analysis of variance. *Educational and Psychological Measurement, 62*(2), 197–226.

Although confidence interval procedures for analysis of variance (ANOVA) have been available for some time, they are not well known and are often difficult to implement with statistical packages. This article discusses procedures for constructing individual and simultaneous confidence intervals on contrasts on parameters of a number of fixed effects ANOVA models, including multivariate analysis of variance (MANOVA) models for the analysis of repeated measures data. Examples demonstrate how these procedures can be implemented with accessible software. Confidence interval inference on parameters of random effects models is also discussed.

Cumming, G., & Finch, S. (2001). A primer on the understanding, use, and calculation of confidence intervals that are based on central and noncentral distributions. *Educational and Psychological Measurement, 61*(4), 532–574.

Reform of statistical practice in the social and behavioral sciences requires wider use of confidence intervals (CIs), effect size measures, and meta-analysis. This article discusses four reasons for using CIs: They (1) are readily interpretable, (2) are linked to familiar statistical significance tests, (3) can encourage meta-analytic thinking, and (4) give information about precision. The authors discuss calculation of CIs for a basic standardized effect size measure, Cohen's d, and contrast these with the familiar CIs for original score means. CIs for d require use of noncentral t distributions, which the authors apply also to statistical power and simple meta-analysis of standardized effect sizes. They provide the ESCI graphical software, which runs under Microsoft Excel, to illustrate the discussion. Wider use of CIs for d and other effect size measures should help promote highly desirable reform of statistical practice in the social sciences.

Fidler, F., & Thompson, B. (2001). Computing correct confidence intervals for ANOVA fixed- and random-effects effect sizes. *Educational and Psychological Measurement, 61*(4), 575–604.

Most textbooks explain how to compute confidence intervals for means, correlation coefficients, and other statistics using "central" test distributions (e.g., *t*, *F*) that are appropriate for such statistics. However, few textbooks explain how to use "noncentral" test distributions (e.g., noncentral *t*, noncentral *F*) to evaluate power or to compute confidence intervals for effect sizes. Illustrates the computation of confidence intervals for effect sizes for some ANOVA applications; the use of intervals invoking noncentral distributions is made practical by newer software. Greater emphasis on both effect sizes and confidence intervals was recommended by the American Psychological Association Task Force on Statistical Inference and is consistent with the editorial policies of the 17 journals that now explicitly require effect size reporting.

Loftus, G. R., & Masson, M. E. J. (1994). Using confidence intervals in within-subject designs. *Psychonomic Bulletin & Review, 1*(4), 476–490.

The authors argue that to best comprehend many data sets, plotting judiciously selected sample statistics with associated confidence intervals can usefully supplement, or even replace, standard hypothesis testing procedures. They describe how to compute an analogous confidence interval that can be used in within-subject designs.

Mendoza, J. L., & Stafford, K. L. (2001). Confidence intervals, power calculation, and sample size estimation for the squared multiple correlation coefficient under the fixed and random regression models: A computer program and useful standard tables. *Educational and Psychological Measurement, 61*(4), 650–667.

This article introduces a computer package written for Mathematica, the purpose of which is to perform a number of difficult iterative functions with respect to the squared multiple correlation coefficient under the fixed and random models. These functions include computation of confidence interval upper and lower bounds, power calculation, calculation of sample size required for a specified power level, and estimating shrinkage in cross-validating the squared multiple correlation under both the random and fixed models. Attention is given to some of the technical issues regarding selecting and working with these two types of models, as well as to issues concerning the construction of confidence intervals.

Smithson, M. (2003). *Confidence intervals.* Thousand Oaks, CA: Sage Publications.

The author first introduces the basis of the confidence interval framework and then provides the criteria for "best" confidence intervals, along with the tradeoffs between confidence and precision. Next, using a reader-friendly style with worked examples from various disciplines, he covers such topics as the relationship between confidence interval and significance testing frameworks, particularly regarding power.

Smithson, M. (2001). Correct confidence intervals for various regression effect sizes and parameters: The importance of noncentral distributions in computing intervals. *Educational and Psychological Measurement, 61* (4), 605–632.

This article provides a practical introduction to methods of constructing confidence intervals for multiple and partial R^2 and related parameters in multiple regression models based on "noncentral" F and X^2 distributions. Until recently, these techniques have not been widely available due to their neglect in popular statistical textbooks and software. These difficulties are addressed here via freely available SPSS scripts and software and illustrations of their use. The article concludes with discussions of implications for the interpretation of findings in terms of noncentral confidence intervals, alternative measures of effect size, the relationship between noncentral confidence intervals and power analysis, and the design of studies.

Steiger, J. H. (2004). Beyond the F test: Effect size, confidence intervals and tests of close fit in the analysis of variance and contrast analysis. *Psychological Methods, 9*(2), 164–182.

The author presents confidence interval methods for improving on the standard F tests in the balanced, completely between-subjects, fixed effects analysis of variance. Exact confidence intervals for omnibus effect size measures, such as ω^2 and the root-mean-square standardized effect, provide all the information in the traditional hypothesis test and more. They allow one to test simultaneously whether overall effects are (a) zero (the traditional test), (b) trivial (do not exceed some small value), or (c) nontrivial (definitely exceed some minimal level). For situations in which single-degree-of-freedom contrasts are of primary interest, exact confidence interval methods for contrast effect size measures such as the contrast correlation are also provided.

Tian, L. (2005). On confidence intervals of a common intraclass correlation coefficient. *Statistics in Medicine, 24,* 3311–3318.

This article presents a novel approach for the confidence interval estimation of a common intraclass correlation coefficient derived from several samples under unequal family sizes. This approach is developed using the concept of generalized pivots. Comparisons are made with a large sample procedure on the coverage probabilities.

Chapter 4. Computer-Intensive Methods

Diaconis, P., & Efron, B. (1983). Computer-intensive methods in statistics. *Scientific American, 48,* 116–130.

This is a classic introduction to this topic.

Software for PCs

Free

- Downloads are available at http://www.tulane.edu/%7Edunlap/ psylib.html for the following programs:

powmr.exe—Computes power for multiple regression

powr.exe—Computes power for simple correlation

power.exe—Computes power for one-way ANOVA

- PINT (Multilevel): http://stat.gamma.rug.nl/Pint_211.zip
- Optimal Design Software (Multilevel): http://sitemaker.umich
.edu/groupbased/files/od156.zip; manual available from: http://
www-personal.umich.edu/~rauden/
- GPower (http://www.psycho.uni-duesseldorf.de/aap/projects/
gpower/), which performs power analyses for some common
statistical tests (t-tests, F-tests, chi-square);
- Mx is a matrix algebra interpreter and numerical optimizer for
structural equation modeling and other types of statistical
modeling of data. The program is available from here: http://
views.vcu.edu/mx/.
- Power and Sample Size (PS) (http://biostat.mc.vanderbilt.edu/
twiki/bin/view/Main/PowerSampleSize); Statistical Power Analysis (http://www.utmb.edu/meo/resource.htm);
- Statistical Power Calculator from: http://www.utmb.edu/meo/
r0000007.exe. Statistical Power Calculator provides statistical
power estimates for a comprehensive range of commonly used
inferential statistics. The package also has utilities for generating critical values for tests of statistical significance, sequences
of random numbers, random sequences for assignment of
participants to independent groups, and the generation of
Latin squares. Finally, the package contains a program that
allows one to conduct Monte Carlo simulations with single-
factor, factorial, and mixed-model analyses of variance. The
programs are suitable for research purposes and as a teaching
tool for students enrolled in statistics and research methods
courses.
- Sample Size for Means (SPSS Syntax File): http://pages.infinit
.net/rlevesqu/Syntax/SampleSize/SampleSizeForMeans.txt
- Sample Size for Proportions (SPSS Syntax File): http://
pages.infinit.net/rlevesqu/Syntax/SampleSize/SampleSizeFor
Proportions.txt

- UnifyPow (SAS module for sample size analysis): http://www .bio.ri.ccf.org/UnifyPow.all/UnifyPow020817a.sas
- Macro-Power and sample size (SAS module for comparing two proportions): http://support.sas.com/faq/042/FAQ04291 .html.

Commercial

- nQuery Advisor: http://www.statsol.ie/
- Power and Precision (logistic regression): http://www.power-analysis.com/
- Statistica Power Analysis: http://www.statsoft.com/products/ power_an.html

The program can compute exact confidence intervals on effect sizes.

- ZumaStat: http://www.zumastat.com/MeansAndANOVA.htm
- PASS: http://www.ncss.com/pass.html
- STATA: http://www.stata.com/
- SAS: http://www.sas.com/
- SPSS: http://www.spss.com/
- S-Plus: http://www.insightful.com/
- SEPATH for STATISTICA software provides SEM with extensive Monte Carlo simulation facilities (http://www.statsoftinc .com/)

World Wide Web Resources

- Effect size calculator for multiple regression: http://www. danielsoper.com/statcalc/calc05.aspx
- A priori sample size calculator for multiple regression: http:// www.danielsoper.com/statcalc/calc01.aspx

- Beta (type II error) calculator: http://www.danielsoper.com/statcalc/calc03.aspx
- Calculator for confidence intervals of relative risk: http://www.hutchon.net/ConfidRR.htm
- Power/sample size calculation for logistic regression with binary covariate(s): http://www.dartmouth.edu/~eugened/power-samplesize.php
- Sample size calculations for logistic regression with exposure measurement error: http://biostat.hitchcock.org/Measurement Error/Analytics/SampleSizeCalculations forLog sticRegression .asp
- VassarStats: http://faculty.vassar.edu/lowry/VassarStats.html
- The following web page computes power, sample size, or minimum detectable odds ratio (OR) for logistic regression with a single binary covariate or two covariates and their interaction: http://www.dartmouth.edu/~eugened/power-samplesize.php
- The following web page provides sample size calculations for logistic regression with a continuous exposure variable and an additional continuous covariate or confounding variable: http://biostat.hitchcock.org/MeasurementError/Analytics/Sample SizeCalculationsforLogisticRegression.asp
  http://faculty.vassar.edu/lowry/VassarStats.html
- A variety of free calculators for determining sample size for two means are available from: http://calculators.stat.ucla.edu/powercalc/
  http://www.sph.emory.edu/~cdckms/samplesize-mean%20 difference.htm
  http://www.changbioscience.com/stat/ssize.html
  http://sampsize.sourceforge.net/iface/s2.html#means
  http://sampsize.sourceforge.net/iface/index.html
  http://www.dssresearch.com/toolkit/sscalc/size.asp
- Sample size for the test of one and two proportions: http://home.ubalt.edu/ntsbarsh/Business-stat/otherapplets/Sample Size.htm#rproptyp
  http://calculators.stat.ucla.edu/powercalc/

http://www.dssresearch.com/toolkit/sscalc/size_p1.asp
http://statpages.org/proppowr.html
• Power analysis for ANOVA designs: http://www.math.yorku
.ca/SCS/Online/power/

This page calculates power or sample size needed to attain a given power for one effect in a factorial ANOVA design. The program was designed to calculate power for a main effect in one-way and two-way factorial designs with fixed effects. However, the program can also be used for *any* fixed effect in *any* crossed factorial design by designating the levels of the effect of interest as A and the levels of all other crossed factors as B.

• Russ Lenth's web page: http://www.stat.uiowa.edu/~rlenth/ Power.

The "balanced ANOVA" selection provides a dialog with a list of several popular experimental designs, plus a provision for specifying your own model.

• The following calculator will tell you the effect size f^2 given a value of R^2: http://www.danielsoper.com/statcalc/calc05.aspx
• Simple Interactive Statistical Analysis (SISA): http://home .clara.net/sisa/correl.htm

Power and sample size for a correlation coefficient.

Notes

Chapter 2

1. The importance of doing a power analysis before beginning a study (prospective power analysis) is universally accepted: such analyses help us to decide how large a sample is required to have a good chance of getting unambiguous results. In contrast, the role of power analysis after the data are collected and analyzed (retrospective power analysis) is controversial. See Baker (1997) and Hoenig and Heisey (2001) for critiques. See Gillett (1996, 2002) for discussions of how to increase the accuracy of retrospective power analysis.

2. Effect size (ES) is a name given to a family of indices that measure the magnitude of a treatment effect. Unlike significance tests, these indices are independent of sample size (Lipsey & Wilson, 1993; Knottnerus & Bouter, 2001). There are a variety of measures of effect size, including the (1) standardized difference between two means (e.g., Cohen's d), (2) correlation between the independent variable and the dependent variable (e.g., Pearson's r), and (3) odds ratio (Rosnow & Rosenthal, 1996). See Huberty (2002) for a review of the history of effect-size indices.

3. Additional information about these packages is available online at http://www.ncss.com/pass.html (PASS); http://www.psycho.uniduesseldorf.de/aap/projects/gpower/ (GPower); http://www.power-analysis.com/specifications.htm (Power and Precision); http://www.stata.com/ (Stata); http://www.sas.com/ (SAS); http://www.insightful.com/ (S-Plus); and http://www.insp.mx/dinf/stat_list.html

(a comprehensive list of power analysis software for PCs). The following texts devote separate chapters to power analysis: Howell (2007), Loftus and Loftus (1988), and Minium and Clarke (1982).

4. There is debate over whether hypothesis testing should focus on accepting or rejecting, as opposed to failing to reject or failing to accept a null hypothesis. For brevity, this discussion adopts the former strategy. See Barnett (1999) for a discussion of alternative approaches to statistical significance.

5. A univariate, normally distributed variable may have either a zero mean or a nonzero mean. If the mean is zero, then we may say that the variable follows a central normal distribution. If the mean is nonzero, then the variable follows a noncentral distribution. Distributions that are derived from normal distributions with nonzero means are called noncentral distributions. For example, in the case of a difference between two means, the quantity d is what most textbooks refer to as a noncentrality parameter. If H_0 states that $m = m_0$, and H_0 is true, then

$$t = \frac{\chi - \mu_0}{s/\sqrt{N}}$$

will be centered about 0. If H_0 is false, then it will not be distributed around 0 because in subtracting m_0 the wrong population mean has been subtracted. In fact, the distribution will be centered at the point

$$t = \frac{\mu_1 - \mu_0}{\sigma/\sqrt{N}}.$$

This shift in the mean of the distribution from 0 to d is referred to as the degree of noncentrality, and d is the noncentrality parameter. The question of power becomes the question of the probability of finding a noncentral (shifted) distribution that is greater than the critical value that t would have under H_0. In other words, even though larger-than-normal values of t are expected because H_0 is false, occasionally small values will be observed by chance. The percentage of these values that lie below the critical value of t is β, the probability of a type II error; and power is equal to $1 - \beta$. Cohen's contribution is splitting the noncentrality parameter d into two parts: sample size and effect size. One part, g, depends solely on parameters of the populations, whereas the other depends on sample size. Thus Cohen separated m_0, m_1, and variance (s), over which there is relatively little control, from sample characteristics (N), over which there is greater control. Although this procedure produces no change in the underlying theory, it makes the concept *d* easier to understand and to use.

6. The terms *random* and *fixed* are used in the context of ANOVA and regression models and refer to assumptions about the independent variable and the error distribution for the variable (Winer, 1971). A "fixed effect" is one that is assumed to be measured without error. It is also assumed that the values of a fixed effect in one study are the same as the values of the fixed variable in another study. "Random effects" are assumed to be values that are drawn from a larger population of values and thus will represent them. The values of random effects represent a random sample of all possible values of that effect. Consequently, the results obtained with a random effect can be generalized to all other possible values of that random variable. Because they involve "inferential leaps," random effects models are less powerful. Random effects models are sometimes referred to as "Model II" or "variance component models." Analyses using both fixed and random effects are called "mixed models."

7. Odds are defined as the chance, for instance, of being in one group versus being in another group. Thus, if in group A 80% are male and 20% female, then the *odds* of being male versus female equal 4; there are four (4.0) times as many males as females. If in group B there are 60% males and 40% females, then in group B the *odds* of being male versus female equal 1.5. The *odds ratio* of A over B equals 2.67 (4.0/1.5), because there are 2.67 more males than females in A than in B.

8. Root mean square error of approximation, RMSEA, is also called RMS or RMSE or discrepancy per degree of freedom. By convention, there is good model fit if RMSEA is less than or equal to .05. There is adequate fit if RMSEA is less than or equal to .08. More recently, Hu and Bentler (1999) have suggested RMSEA $\leq$ .06 as the cutoff for a good model fit. RMSEA is a popular measure of fit, partly because it does not require comparison with a null model and thus does not require the author to posit as plausible a model in which there is complete independence of the latent variables as does, for instance, comparative fit index (CFI). Also, RMSEA has a known distribution, related to the noncentral chi-square distribution, and thus does not require bootstrapping to establish confidence intervals. Confidence intervals for RMSEA are reported by some statistical packages. It is one of the fit indexes less affected by sample size, though for smallest sample sizes it overestimates goodness of fit (Fan, Thompson, & Wang, 1999). RMSEA is computed as $((\text{chisq}/((n-1)df)) - (df/((n-1)df)))^*.5$, where chisq is model chi-square, df is the degrees of freedom, and n is number of participants.

Chapter 4

1. Information about Resampling Stats is located at http://www.resample.com/.

2. http://pages.infinit.net/rlevesqu/index.htm for SPSS and http://support.sas.com/ctx/samples/index.jsp for SAS.

3. For David Howell's software see: http://www.uvm.edu/~dhowell/StatPages/Resampling/Resampling.html.

References

Adcock, C. J. (1997). Sample size determination: A review. *Statistician, 46*(2), 261–283.

Algina, J., & Keselman, H. J. (2003). Approximate confidence intervals for effect sizes. *Educational and Psychological Measurement, 63*(4), 537–553.

Algina, J., & Moulder, B. C. (2001). Sample sizes for confidence intervals on the increase in the squared multiple correlation coefficient. *Educational and Psychological Measurement, 61*(4), 633–649.

Algina, J., & Olejnik, S. (2000). Determining sample size for accurate estimation of the squared multiple correlation coefficient. *Multivariate Behavioral Research, 35*(1), 119–137.

Algina, J., & Olejnik, S. (2003). Sample size tables for correlation analysis with applications in partial correlation and multiple regression analysis. *Multivariate Behavioral Research, 38*(3), 309–323.

Allison, D. B., Allison, R. L., Faith, M. S., Paultre, F., & Pi-sunyer, F. X. (1997). Power and money: Designing statistically powerful studies while minimizing financial costs. *Psychological Methods, 2*(1), 20–33

Assman, S. F., Pocock, S. J., Enos, L. E., & Kasten, L. E. (2000). Subgroup analysis and other (mis)uses of baseline data in clinical trials. *Lancet, 355*, 1064–1069.

Bacchetti, P., Wolf, L. E., Segal, M. R., & McCulloch, C. E. (2005a). Ethics and sample size. *American Journal of Epidemiology, 161*(2), 105–110.

Bacchetti, P., Wolf, L. E., Segal, M. R., & McCulloch, C. E. (2005b). Bacchetti, et al. respond to "Ethics and sample size—Another view." *American Journal of Epidemiology, 161*(2), 113.

Baker, L. (1997). Retrospective power analysis. *Conservation Biology, 11*(1), 276–280.

Bannister, D. (1981) Personal construct theory and research method. In P. Reason & J. Rowan (Eds.), *Human inquiry* (pp. 191–199). Chichester, England: Wiley.

Barnett, V. (1999). *Comparative statistical inference.* New York: Wiley.

Barnette, J. (2005). ScoreRel CI: Software for computation of confidence intervals for commonly used score reliability coefficients. *Educational and Psychological Measurement, 65,* 980–983.

Betensky, R. A. (1997). Conditional power calculations for early acceptance of H_0 embedded in sequential trials. *Statistics in Medicine, 16*(4), 465–477.

Bird, K. D. (2002). Confidence intervals for effect sizes in analysis of variance. *Educational and Psychological Measurement, 62*(2), 197–226.

Borenstein, M. (1994). The case for confidence intervals in controlled clinical trials. *Controlled Clinical Trials, 15*(5), 411–428.

Browne, M. W., & Cudeck, R. (1993). Alternative ways of assessing model fit. In K. A. Bollen & J. S. Long (Eds.), *Testing structural models* (pp. 136–162). Newbury Park, CA: Sage.

Campbell, M. J, Julious, S. A., & Altman, D. G. (1995). Estimating sample sizes for binary, ordered categorical and continuous outcomes in two group comparisons. *British Medical Journal, 311,* 1145–1148.

Cohen, J. (1962). The statistical power of abnormal-social psychological research: A review. *Journal of Abnormal and Social Psychology, 65,* 145–153.

Cohen, J. (1969). *Statistical power analysis for the behavioral sciences.* New York: Academic Press.

Cohen, J. (1977). *Statistical power analysis for the behavioral sciences.* New York: Academic Press.

Cohen, J. (1988). *Statistical power analysis for the behavioral sciences* (2nd ed.). Hillsdale, NJ: Erlbaum.

Cohen, J. (1992). A power primer. *Psychological Bulletin, 112,* 155–159.

Cohen, J. (1994). The earth is round ($p < .05$). *American Psychologist, 49*(12), 997–102.

Cohen, J., & Cohen, P. (1983). *Applied multiple regression/correlation analysis for the behavioral sciences.* Hillsdale, NJ: Erlbaum.

Cochran, W. G. (1977). Sampling techniques. New York: Wiley.

Cook, T. D., & Campbell, D. T. (1979). *Quasi-experimentation: Design and analysis issues for field settings.* Boston: Houghton Mifflin.

Cox, D. R., & Oakes, D. (2001). *Analysis of survival data.* London: Chapman & Hall.

Cuddeback, G., Wilson, E., Orme, J. G., & Combs-Orme, T. (2004). Detecting and statistically correcting sample selection bias. *Journal of Social Service Research, 30*(3), 19–33.

Cumming, G., & Finch, S. (2001). A primer on the understanding, use, and calculation of confidence intervals that are based on central and non-central distributions. *Educational and Psychological Measurement, 61*(4), 532–574.

D'Amico, E. J., Neilands T. B., & Zambarano, R. (2001). Power analysis for multivariate and repeated measures designs: A flexible approach using the SPSS MANOVA procedure. *Behavior Research Methods, Instruments, and Computers, 33*(4), 479–484.

Daniel, W. W., & Terrel, J. C. (1992). *Business statistics for management and economics.* Boston: Houghton Mifflin.

Darlington, R. B. (1990). *Regression and linear models.* New York: McGraw-Hill.

Diaconis, P., & Efron, B. (1983). Computer-intensive methods in statistics. *Scientific American, 48,* 116–130.

Edington, E. S. (1995). *Randomization tests.* New York: Dekker.

Efron, B. (1979). Bootstrap methods: Another look at the jackknife. *Annals of Statistics, 7,* 1–26.

Efron, B. (1982). *The jackknife, the bootstrap and other resampling plans.* Philadelphia: Society for Industrial and Applied Mathematics.

Efron, B., & Tibshirani, R. J. (1993). *An introduction to the bootstrap.* New York: Chapman & Hall.

Enders, C. K. (2003). Performing multivariate group comparisons following a statistically significant MANOVA. *Measurement and Evaluation in Counseling and Development, 36,* 40–56.

Fan, X., Thompson, B., & Wang, L. (1999). The effects of sample size, estimation methods, and model specification on SEM fit indices. *Structural Equation Modeling: A Multidisciplinary Journal, 6,* 56–83.

Fidler, F., & Thompson, B. (2001). Computing correct confidence intervals for ANOVA fixed- and random-effects effect sizes. *Educational and Psychological Measurement, 61*(4), 575–604.

Fink, A. (2002). *How to sample in surveys* (Vol. 7). Thousand Oaks, CA: Sage.

Fisher, R. A. (1925). *Statistical methods for research workers.* Edinburgh, UK: Oliver & Boyd.

Fleishman, A. I. (1980). Confidence intervals for correlation ratios. *Educational and Psychological Measurement, 40,* 659–670.

Fleiss, J. L., Levin, B., & Paik, C. M. (2003). *Statistical methods for rates and proportions.* Hoboken, NJ: Wiley.

Frick, R. W. (1995). A problem with confidence intervals. *American Psychologist, 50,* 1102–1103.

Gastonis, C., & Sampson, A. R. (1989). Multiple correlation: Exact power and sample size calculations. *Psychological Bulletin, 106*(3), 516–524.

Gill, J. (2002). *Bayesian methods: A social and behavioral sciences approach.* New York: Chapman & Hall.

Gillett, R. (1996). Retrospective power surveys. *Statistician, 45,* 231–236.

Gillett, R. (2002). The unseen power loss: Stemming the flow. *Educational and Psychological Measurement, 62,* 960–968.

Glass, G. V. (1976). Primary, secondary, and meta-analysis of research. *Educational Researcher, 5,* 3–8.

Glass, G. V., McGaw, B., & Smith, M. L. (1981). *Meta-analysis in social research.* Beverly Hills, CA: Sage.

Good, P. (1999). *Resampling methods: A practical guide to data analysis.* Boston: Birkhäuser.

Guo, S., & Hussey, D. L. (2004). Nonprobability sampling in social work research: Dilemmas, consequences, and strategies. *Journal of Social Service Research, 30*(3), 1–18.

Hager, W., & Möller, H. (1986). Tables and procedures for the determination of power and sample sizes in univariate and multivariate analyses of variance and regression. *Biometrical Journal, 28,* 647–663.

Hancock, G. R., & Freeman, M. J. (2001). Power and sample size for the root mean square error of approximation test of not close fit in structural equation modeling. *Educational and Psychological Measurement, 61*(5), 741–758.

Harrell, F. E. (1984). Regression modeling strategies for improved prognostic prediction. *Statistics in Medicine, 3,* 143–152.

Hedges, L. V., & Olkin, I. (1985). *Statistical methods for meta-analysis.* San Diego, CA: Academic Press.

Helberg, C. (1996). Pitfalls of data analysis. *Practical Assessment, Research and Evaluation, 5*(5). Retrieved July 18, 2006, from http://PAREonline.net/getvn.asp?v=5&n=5

Henry, G. (1990). *Practical sampling.* Newbury Park, CA: Sage.

Hinkle, D. E., Wiersma, W., & Jurs, S. G. (2003). *Applied statistics in the social sciences.* Boston: Houghton Mifflin.

Hoenig, J. M., & Heisey, D. M. (2001). The abuse of power: The pervasive fallacy of power calculations for data analysis. *American Statistician, 55,* 19–24.

Howell, D. C. (2007). *Statistical methods for psychology* (6th ed.). Belmont, CA: Wadsworth.

Hox, J. J. (2002). *Multilevel analysis: Techniques and applications.* Mahwah, NJ: Erlbaum.

Hoyle, R. H. (1999). *Statistical strategies for small sample research.* Thousand Oaks, CA: Sage.

Hsieh, F. Y. (1989). Sample size tables for logistic regression. *Statistics in Medicine, 8,* 795–802.

Hsieh, F. Y., Bloch, D. A., & Larsen, M. D. (1998). A simple method of sample size calculation for linear and logistic regression. *Statistics in Medicine, 17*(1), 623–634.

Hsieh, F. Y., Lavori, P. W., Cohen, H. J., & Feussner, J. R. (2003). An overview of variance inflation factors for sample-size calculation. *Evaluation and the Health Professions, 26*(3), 239–257.

Hu, L., & Bentler, P. M. (1999). Cutoff criteria for fit indexes in covariance structure analysis: Conventional criteria versus new alternatives. *Structural Equation Modeling, 6,* 1–55.

Huberty, C. J. (1993). Historical origins of statistical testing practices: The treatment of Fisher versus Neyman-Pearson views in textbooks. *Journal of Experimental Education, 61,* 317–333.

Huberty, C. J. (2002). A history of effect size indices. *Educational and Psychological Measurement, 62*(2), 227–240.

Huberty, C. J., & Morris, J. D. (1989). Multivariate analysis versus multiple univariate analyses. *Psychological Bulletin, 105,* 305–308.

Hunter, J. E., Schmidt, F. L., & Jackson, G. B. (1982). *Meta-analysis: Cumulating research findings across studies.* Beverly Hills, CA: Sage.

Isaac, S., & Michael, W. B. (1995). *Handbook in research and evaluation.* San Diego, CA: EdITS.

Kirk, R. E. (1996). Practical significance: A concept whose time has come. *Educational and Psychological Measurement, 56,* 746–759.

Kish, L. (1965). *Survey sampling.* New York: Wiley.

Klein, K., & Kozlowski, S. W. (Eds.). (2000). *Multilevel theory, research, and methods in organizations.* San Francisco: Jossey-Bass.

Knottnerus, J. A., & Bouter, L. M. (2001). The ethics of sample size: Two-sided testing and one-sided thinking. *Journal of Clinical Epidemiology, 54,* 109–110.

Kraemer, H. C., & Thiemann S. (1987). *How many subjects? Statistical power analysis in research.* Newbury Park, CA: Sage.

Kreft, I. (1996). *Are multilevel techniques necessary? An overview, including simulation studies.* Retrieved July 9, 2006, from http://www.calstatela.edu/faculty/ikreft/quarterly/quarterly.html

Kruglanski, A. W. (1975). The endogenous-exogeneous partition in attribution theory. *Psychological Review, 82,* 387–406.

Kupper, L. L., & Hafner, K. B. (1989). How appropriate are sample size formulas? *American Statistician, 43*(2), 101–105.

Lachin, J. M. (2005). A review of methods for futility stopping based on conditional power. *Statistics in Medicine, 24,* 2747–2764.

Laudan, L. (1977). *Progress and its problem: Towards a theory of scientific growth.* Berkeley, CA: University of California Press.

Lê, T., & Verma, V. (1997). *An analysis of sampling designs and sampling errors of the demographic and health surveys* [Report No. AR3]. Calverton, MD: Macro International.

Lenth, R. V. (2001). Some practical guidelines for effective sample-size determination. *American Statistician, 55*(3), 187–193.

Lipsey, M. W. (1990). *Design sensitivity: Statistical power for experimental research.* Newbury Park, CA: Sage.

Lipsey, M. W., & Wilson, D. B. (1993). The efficacy of psychological, educational, and behavioral treatment: Confirmation from meta-analysis. *American Psychologist, 48*, 1181–1209.

Loftus, G. R., & Loftus, E. F. (1988). *Essentials of statistics.* New York: Random House.

Loftus, G. R., & Masson, M. E. J. (1994). Using confidence intervals in within-subject designs. *Psychonomic Bulletin and Review, 1*(4), 476–490.

Ludbrook, J., & Dudley, H. (1998). Why permutation tests are superior to *t* and *F* tests in biomedical research. *American Statistician, 52*, 127–132.

Lunneborg, C. E. (2000). *Data analysis by resampling: Concepts and applications.* Belmont, CA: Duxbury Press.

MacCallum, R. C., Browne, M. W., & Sugawara, H. M. (1996). Power analysis and determination of sample size for covariance structure modeling. *Psychological Methods, 1*, 130–149.

Maxwell, S. E. (2000). Sample size and multiple regression analysis. *Psychological Methods, 5*(4), 434–458.

McClelland, G. H. (1997). Optimal design in psychological research. *Psychological Methods, 2*(1), 3–19.

Mendoza, J. L., & Stafford, K. L. (2001). Confidence intervals, power calculation, and sample size estimation for the squared multiple correlation coefficient under the fixed and random regression models: A computer program and useful standard tables. *Educational and Psychological Measurement, 61*(4), 650–667.

Minium, E. W., & Clarke, R. B. (1982). *Elements of statistical reasoning.* New York: Wiley.

Muller, K. E., LaVange, L. M., Ramey, S. L., & Ramey, C. T. (1992). Power calculations for general linear multivariate models including repeated measures applications. *Journal of the American Statistical Association, 87*, 1209–1226.

Muthen, B., & Satorra, A. (1995). Complex sample data in structural equation modeling. In P. V. Marsden (Ed.), *Sociological methodology* (pp. 267–316). Oxford, England: Blackwell.

Murphy, K., & Myors, B. (2003). *Statistical power analysis: A simple and general model for traditional and modern hypothesis tests* (2nd ed.). Mahwah, NJ: Erlbaum.

Neale, M. C., Boker, S. M., Xie, G., & Maes, H. H. (1999). *Mx executables.* Retrieved August 21, 2006 from http://www.vcu.edu/mx/executables.html

Neyman, J. (1952). *Lectures and conferences on mathematical statistics and probability.* Washington, DC: U.S. Department of Agriculture.

Neyman, J., & Pearson, E. S. (1928). On the use and interpretation of certain test criteria for purposes of statistical inferences (Part 1). *Biometrika, 20A,* 175–240.

Noreen, E. (1989). *Computer-intensive methods for testing hypotheses.* New York: Wiley.

Orme, J. G., & Hudson, W. W. (1995). The problem of sample size estimation: Confidence intervals. *Social Work Research, 19*(2), 121–127.

Parker, R. A., & Berman, N. G. (2003). Sample size: More than calculations. *The American Statistician, 57*(3), 166–170.

Pearson, E. S., & Please, N. W. (1975). Relationship between the shape of population distribution and robustness or four simple testing statistics. *Biometrika, 62,* 223–241.

Peterson, I. (1991). Pick a sample. *Science News.* Retrieved August 9, 2006, from http://www.resample.com/content/teaching/texts/picksample.txt

Peterson, R. S., Smith, B. D., & Martorana, P. V. (2006). Choosing between a rock and a hard place when data are scarce and questions important: A reply to Hooenbeck, DeRue, and Mannor (2006). *Journal of Applied Psychology, 9*(1), 6–8.

Pocock, S. J., Geller, N. L., & Tsiatis, A. A. (1987). The analysis of multiple endpoints in clinical trials. *Biometrics, 43,* 487–498.

Posch, M., & Bauer, P. (2000). Interim analysis and sample size reassessment. *Biometrics, 56*(4), 1170–1176.

Prentice, R. (2005). Invited commentary: Ethics and sample size—Another view. *American Journal of Epidemiology, 161*(2), 111–112.

Rodgers, J. L. (1999). The bootstrap, the jackknife, and the randomization test: A sample taxonomy. *Multivariate Behavioral Research, 34,* 441–456.

Rosnow, R. L., & Rosenthal, R. (1996). Computing contrasts, effect sizes, and counternulls on other people's published data: General procedures for research consumers. *Psychological Methods, 1,* 331–340.

Rubin, A., & Babbie, E. R. (2005). *Research methods for social work.* Belmont, CA: Brooks/Cole.

Rudner, L. M., & Shafer, M. M. (1992). Resampling: A marriage of computers and statistics. *Practical Assessment, Research and Evaluation, 3*(5). Retrieved July 17, 2006, from http://PAREonline.net/getvn.asp?v=3&n=5

Satorra, A., & Saris, W. E. (1985). Power of the likelihood ratio test in covariance structure analysis. *Psychometrika, 50,* 83–90.

Schechtman, K. B., & Gordon, M. E. (1993). A comprehensive algorithm for determining whether a run-in strategy will be a cost-effective design modification in a randomized clinical trial. *Statistics in Medicine, 12,* 111–128.

Schmidt, F. L., & Hunter, J. E. (1997). Eight common but false objections to the discontinuation of significance testing in the analysis of research data. In L. L. Harlow, S. A. Mulaik, & J. H. Steiger (Eds.), *What if there were no significance tests?* (pp. 37–64). Mahwah, NJ: Erlbaum.

Shih, W. J. (2001). Sample size re-estimation: Journey for a decade. *Statistics in Medicine, 20,* 515–518.

Smithson, M. (2001). Correct confidence intervals for various regression effect sizes and parameters: The importance of noncentral distributions in computing intervals. *Educational and Psychological Measurement, 61*(4), 605–632.

Smithson, M. (2003). *Confidence intervals.* Thousand Oaks, CA: Sage.

Snijders, T. A., & Bosker, R. J. (1993). Standard errors and sampling sizes for two-level research. *Journal of Educational Statistics, 18,* 237–261.

Sprent, P. (1998). *Data driven statistical methods.* London: Chapman & Hall.

Steiger, J. H. (2004). Beyond the F-test: Effect size confidence intervals and tests of close fit in the analysis of variance and contrast analysis. *Psychological Methods, 9* (2), 164–182.

Steiger, J. H. (2000) Point estimation, hypothesis testing, and interval estimation using the RMSEA: Some comments and a reply to Hayduk and Glaser. *Structural Equation Modeling, 7,* 149–162.

Steiger, J. H. (1990). Structural model evaluation and modifications: An interval estimation approach. *Multivariate Behavioral Research, 25,* 173–180.

Steiger, J. H., & Fouladi, R. T. (1992). R2: A computer program for interval estimation, power calculation, and hypothesis testing for the squared multiple correlation. *Behavior Research Methods, Instruments, and Computers, 4,* 581–582.

Stevens, J. (2002). *Applied multivariate statistics for the social sciences.* Mahwah, NJ: Erlbaum.

Stine, R. (1989). An introduction to bootstrap methods: Examples and ideas. *Sociological Methods and Research, 8*(2 & 3), 243–290.

Tabachnick, B. G., & Fidell, L. S. (2001). *Using multivariate statistics* (4th ed.). New York: HarperCollins.

Tian, L. (2005). On confidence intervals of a common intraclass correlation coefficient. *Statistics in Medicine, 24,* 3311–3318.

Thompson, B. (2002). What future quantitative social science research could look like: Confidence intervals for effect sizes. *Educational Researcher, 31*(3), 25–32.

Thompson, B., & Snyder, P. A. (1997). Statistical significance testing practices in the *Journal of Experimental Education*. *Journal of Experimental Education, 66*, 75–83.

Tukey, J. W. (1991). Bias and confidence in not-quite large samples. In C. L. Mallow, (Ed.), *The collected works of John W. Tukey VI, more mathematical: 1938–1984* (pp. 391–393). Monterey, CA: Wadsworth.

Vaeth, M., & Skovlund, E. (2004). A simple approach to power and sample size calculations in logistic regression and Cox regression models. *Statistics in Medicine, 23*(11), 1781–1792.

van Belle, G. (2002). *Statistical rules of thumb*. New York: Wiley.

Walters, S. J. (2004). Sample size and power estimation for studies with health related quality of life outcomes: A comparison of four methods using the SF-36. *Health and Quality of Life Outcomes, 2*. Retrieved July 2, 2006, from http://www.hqlo.com/content/2/1/26

Whitehead, J. (1997). *The design and analysis of sequential clinical trials*. Chichester, England: Wiley.

Whittemore, A. S. (1981). Sample size for logistic regression with small response probability. *Journal of the American Statistical Association, 76*, 27–32.

Winer, B. J. (1971). *Statistical principles in experimental designs*. New York: McGraw-Hill.

Winship, C., & Marc, R. (1992). Models for sample selection bias. *Annual Review of Sociology, 18*, 327–350.

Whitley, E., & Ball, J. (2002). Statistics review 4: Sample size calculations. *Critical Care, 6*, 335–341.

Wuensch, K. (2006). Power analysis for an analysis of covariance. Retrieved August 7, 2006, from http://core.ecu.edu/psyc/wuenschk/MV/LSANOVA/Power-ANCOV.doc

Zimmerman, D. (2004). A note on preliminary tests of equality of variances. *British Journal of Mathematical and Statistical Psychology, 57*, 173–181.

Index